LINCOLN CHRISTIAN COLLEGE

REDEEMING POP CULTURE

REDEEMING POP CULTURE

A Kingdom Approach

T. M. MOORE

P&R
PUBLISHING
P.O. BOX 817 • PHILLIPSBURG • NEW JERSEY 08865-0817

© 2003 by T. M. Moore

All rights reserved. No part of this book may be reproduced, stored in a retrieval system, or transmitted in any form or by any means—electronic, mechanical, photocopy, recording, or otherwise—except for brief quotations for the purpose of review or comment, without the prior permission of the publisher, P&R Publishing Company, P.O. Box 817, Phillipsburg, New Jersey 08865-0817.

All Scripture quotations are from the King James Version.

Page design by Tobias Design
Typesetting by Michelle Feaster

Printed in the United States of America

Library of Congress Cataloging-in-Publication Data

Moore, T. M. (Terry Michael), 1949-
Redeeming pop culture : a kingdom approach / T. M. Moore.
p. cm.
Includes bibliographical references.
ISBN 0-87552-576-8 (pbk.)
1. Popular culture—Religious aspects—Christianity. 2. Christianity and culture—United States. 3. Popular culture—United States. 4. United States—Church history. I. Title.

BR115.C8M66 2003
261—dc21

2003048225

For Kevin, Kristy, Ashley, and Casey

But seek ye first the kingdom of God,
and his righteousness.
—Matthew 6:33

Contents

Introduction

Everything Kudzu
A Nightmare

Last night I was in the weirdest specialty store
where anything you wanted you could buy,
as long as it was kudzu. There were more

things made of kudzu than I'd even try
to tell, and all the aisles were filled with folk,
all busy filling shopping carts sky high

with everything kudzu. I thought, Is this a joke?
Is this some hidden camera prank on me?
A woman stood before a mirror and stroked

her kudzu wig with a kudzu brush. "I'll see
this in a smaller size," she told the girl,
and stepped aside to let a man with three

large bags of kudzu groceries squeeze by her.
In another aisle a man was looking at
some kudzu boots, while a woman in a fur

coat made of kudzu sought a kudzu hat
to match. “Attention, Kudzu shoppers,” came
a voice from somewhere. “Please remember that

it’s bonus day. So have your Kudzu Game
Cards ready at the Kudzu checkout lane
to validate your membership and claim

your Kudzu prize.” A cheer went up like a chain
reaction throughout the kudzu store. I must
be crazy; yes, I’ve surely gone insane,

I thought. “Oh look at this! Now isn’t this just
the kudzu cutest?” a woman in a vest
of kudzu standing near me asked. “I trust

he’ll like it. Tell me what you think.” I guessed
that she was asking me, and turned to see
what she was holding, when all at once the rest

of the shoppers in the store all wanted me
to look at their prospective purchases
as well, and crowded close for me to see

their kudzu junk, but every item was
the same. The more they pressed on me, the more
they seemed to blend together in a fuzz

and blur of kudzu. Get out of this crazy store,
I told myself, before you suffocate!
But I was blocked on every side, no door

in sight. "Attention, Kudzu shoppers . . ." Great
green kudzu tendrils reached for me as the voice
on the intercom grew louder. "Half past eight . . ."

The crowd was in a frenzied row; the noise
was deafening. I heard, "Here's the traffic now
with Sandy." Gasping and flailing, I was poised

to be overcome by kudzu. When somehow,
I awoke, alarmed, sweat pouring from my brow.

For many Americans, popular culture has become a nightmare, a bad dream that gets worse and worse as the night goes on, disturbing their peace and filling them with dread. Parents wring their hands over their children's language and their taste in music and fashion. Moralists declaim against the "culture of violence" that captures the imagination of young children in cartoons and video games and turns them into schoolyard shooters before they reach high school. Social theorists defend the right of pop artists to extol the virtues of free sex—to the dismay of traditionalists—while, at the same time, angrily pressing governments to fund preventive measures against STDs and unwanted pregnancies. Literary purists decry the popularity of romance novels as threatening to destroy literature altogether. Politicians summon producers of popular culture to highly publicized hearings and demand more responsible approaches to the publication of music lyrics and the production of films and television shows. Religious leaders rail against the music, film, and

TV industries, charging them with debasing the culture and morals of the land. Around the community, leaders lament the inundation of popular culture as it rises inexorably around us—even as they settle in to watch their favorite evening sitcoms.

Not long ago, I sat with my family in a restaurant on the north bank of the Tennessee River in downtown Knoxville. I looked out across the water to where a sturdy stand of kudzu decorated the opposite bank and protected the structures above it from erosion. It was a lovely sight, but one that, I'm sure, has to be constantly maintained, lest the kudzu climb the fence, invade the grounds beyond, and threaten to overwhelm everything on the property, as it has done in so many parts of the rural South.

Popular culture in America has become like kudzu, the tenacious southern vine. While it has certain intrinsic properties of beauty and functionality, and is therefore desirable, it can overgrow and overwhelm everything in its path when left unchecked, turning whole forests, fields, and farms into an indistinguishable kudzu chaos. As controlling the kudzu has become a challenge to every southern farmer, so controlling the themes, styles, availability, and effects of popular culture has taken on a sense of urgency for a great many Americans.

The purpose of this book is to provide guidance for evangelical Christians in dealing with popular culture in a way that fosters appreciation for it and even enjoyment of it, without compromising Christ's call to seek first the kingdom of God and His righteousness. Ken Myers has written, "I believe that *the challenge of living with popular culture* may well be as serious for modern Christians as persecution and plagues were for the saints of earlier centuries."[1] This book is an attempt to help evangelicals understand, cope with, and even benefit from the popular culture that every day confronts and challenges them as they pursue their mission in the kingdom of Christ.

Before we begin to examine the distinctive character of popular culture and to formulate a biblical approach to dealing with it, it will help us to understand some of the other ways people relate to this phenomenon today, and to consider how popular culture works for the individual "consumer."

Approaches to Popular Culture

A great many approaches to understanding and relating to popular culture are currently being followed.[2] Four of these in particular are of interest to our study. The first is what we might call a *phenomenological* approach. Proponents of this approach seek merely to acknowledge the fact of popular culture and to examine particular expressions of it. The phenomenological approach offers little in the way of criticism, celebration, or warning; instead, its purpose is merely to describe popular culture as a fact of American life. This is the approach taken by such popular newsweeklies as *Time* and *U.S. News & World Report.* Brief reports on music, film, television, literature, sports, and other aspects of popular culture are put forward in a relatively nonjudgmental manner, primarily to inform readers of the latest developments, fashions, and fads.

A second approach to popular culture is what might be called the *celebratory* approach. This approach emphasizes the positive value of particular expressions of popular culture as sources of meaning and gratification. A celebratory approach will most often be found among groups of "fans," where devotees of one or another segment of the popular culture enjoy, often together, the benefits they receive from their particular diversion. This is what we find happening at a professional baseball game, among the subscribers to *Entertainment Weekly,* at a rock concert, or even in a reading group at a local bookstore. The celebratory approach entails aspects of the phenomenological, but goes far beyond it to include critical reflection and comparison, although only within the specific segment of popular culture to which the devotees are committed.[3]

A third approach we might call *ideological.* An ideological approach to popular culture seeks to be more analytical, trying to decipher the messages and meanings of the various expressions of popular culture at an abstract level. While all consumers of popular culture are concerned with messages and meanings, most often these are appropriated in highly individualized ways, according to personal tastes and values, as we shall see. Those who take an ideological approach to popular culture are more concerned with the general or universal messages and meanings in any particular form. This is the approach we see in a book like Thomas S. Hibbs's *Shows About Nothing,*[4] or in James Bowman's essays on the media in *The New Criterion.*

A fourth approach to popular culture we may call *moral.* Those who take a moral approach to popular culture avail themselves of the methods of all the other approaches, but go beyond these to issue warnings and recommendations about particular artifacts and forms of popular culture, especially as these may exert influence on attitudes and behavior. Those who take a moral approach to popular culture will support the inclusion of warning labels on certain kinds of recordings or a rating system for television and film. Christian publications and organizations—such as *World* and Focus on the Family—tend to take a moralist approach to their reviews of aspects of the popular culture, recommending certain forms and warning against the negative effects of others.

Anyone who interacts with popular culture will recognize one or more of these four approaches in his or her own efforts to make sense of this phenomenon.

A Biblical Approach to Popular Culture

None of these approaches to popular culture exists in a pure form. Rather, each partakes of aspects of the others to a certain extent. A biblical approach, however, must go further. Certainly a biblical approach to popular culture will involve all of these approaches. Those using a biblical approach will want, like good sons and daughters of Issachar,[5] to be alert to developments in the popular culture. Thus, they will keep abreast of trends, artists, and productions and try to describe them as fully as possible (the phenomenological approach). Those who follow a biblical approach will certainly extol certain aspects of the popular culture, as evangelicals generally have done with television programs like *Touched by an Angel* and films like *Chariots of Fire* and *The Patriot* (the celebratory approach). Here they must seek to "hold fast to what is good" in popular culture.[6] A biblical approach will necessarily be ideological in its relationship to popular culture, seeking to determine the overt and covert messages of various cultural forms, as well as pointing out their universal significance. This is part of the evangelical calling to "discern the spirits."[7] Further, a biblical approach to popular culture must not shy away from the moral duty of exposing what is evil or what threatens to bring harm to individuals or society.[8] This moral or prophetic role is an essential aspect of the evangelical's calling in the kingdom of God.

Thus, all the approaches that we have mentioned above will be included in a biblical approach to popular culture. However, while a proper biblical approach will involve all of these, it will go one step further to include a *missiological* element as well. This requires evangelicals to relate to popular culture in such a way as to carry out the evangelical mission of proclaiming and embodying the kingdom of God. Here the objective is to take popular culture captive, so to speak, in ways that will allow evangelicals to enjoy and use it in service to the kingdom purposes of Jesus Christ.[9] A biblical approach to popular culture is part of both the Great Commission and the cultural mandate, twin aspects of the Christian's calling to make disciples in every nation.[10] The distinctive elements of this biblical—or, better, kingdom—approach to popular culture will be spelled out more fully in chapter 5, although they are suggested throughout the book.

The Appeal of Popular Culture

One reason why it is so important for evangelicals—indeed, for all Americans—to understand popular culture is that it is so popular. As we will see in chapter 1, popular culture is *the* distinctively American culture. More than any other cultural expression, it reaches, embraces, enthralls, and influences the largest portion of the American public. Anything that captures the hearts and imaginations of so many people, and with so much passion and intensity, should certainly be of concern to evangelical Christians.

How does popular culture accomplish this? What makes it so popular?

Popular culture works by appealing above all to the affections—what Jonathan Edwards defined as "the more vigorous and sensible exercises of the inclination and will of the soul."[11] He goes on to say:

> In every thing we do, wherein we act voluntarily, there is an exercise of the will and inclination; it is our inclination that governs us in our actions; but all the actings of the inclination and will, in all our common actions of life, are not ordinarily called affections. Yet what are commonly called affections are most essentially different from them, but only in the degree and manner of exercise. In every act of the will whatsoever, the soul either likes or dislikes, is either inclined or disinclined to what is in view: these are not essentially different from those

> affections of love and hatred. That liking or inclination of the soul to a thing, if it be in a high degree, and be vigorous and lively, is the very same thing with the affection of love; and that disliking and disinclining if in a great degree, is the very same with hatred. In every act of the will for or towards something not present, the soul is in some degree inclined to that thing; and that inclination, if in a considerable degree, is the very same with the affection of desire. And in every degree of the act of the will, wherein the soul approves of something present, there is a degree of pleasedness; and that pleasedness, if it be in a considerable degree, is the very same with the affections of joy or delight.[12]

Affections are thus the deep inclinations, aspirations, and resonating points of the soul. The affection to which popular culture most consistently appeals is pleasure[13]—what Edwards called "pleasedness." Artifacts and forms of popular culture continue to abound—and the producers of them continue to prosper—because they bring pleasure to those who consume them. As John Fiske observes (referring to the forms of popular culture as "texts"),

> The popular text must align itself with the tastes and concerns of its readers, not its author, if the readers are to choose it from the wide repertoire of other texts available: it must offer inviting access to the pleasures and meanings it may provide.[14]

As soon as a form ceases to give pleasure, consumers move on to other forms and artifacts. This explains, among other things, the constantly changing lists of rock and movie hits and the generally ephemeral character of popular culture as a whole (see chapter 1).

Popular culture experiments with an unending variety of forms and artifacts in order to discover which ones will provide the greatest pleasure for the largest number of consumers. For every hit record released, scores of failures are withdrawn. For every popular film or television program, dozens more are taken off the air or out of circulation. Producers of popular culture work hard to discover consumer "interests" and "needs" before they invest in different artifacts and forms. Telephone surveys, focus groups, and demographic studies are just a few of the methods employed to help ensure that producers reap maximum financial rewards by providing pleasure to the maximum number of consumers.

All this sounds rather crass and commercial, and, indeed, much of popular culture is precisely that—especially since it can claim to provide no more than a highly individualized form of pleasure.

However, pleasure in and of itself is not bad. God apparently took great pleasure in the cosmos He created, since we see Him often reflecting with satisfaction on the "good" creation in Genesis 1. He takes pleasure as well in those who fear Him, as Psalm 147:10-11 suggests. Thus, appealing to pleasure and seeking to gratify pleasure are not necessarily bad or evil ends. Pleasure can be a valid affection, and, to the extent that it is, people ought to cultivate it to a high degree of fulfillment.

The problem with popular culture is not its appeal to

pleasure. Rather, it is the *definition* of pleasure that prevails within American culture and society today. In our postmodern environment, the only valid pleasure is that which provides individual gratification, individually defined. Thus, one man's pleasure, to paraphrase an old saw, may well be another man's poison. In the postmodern world, personal identity and gratification are secured within the context of groups or subcultures–what John Frow calls "regimes of value."[15] These regimes of value define what is important for the members of an individual subculture.

> The concept of regime expresses one of the fundamental theses of work in cultural studies: that no object, no text, no cultural practice has an intrinsic or necessary meaning or value or function; and that meaning, value, and function are always the effect of specific (and changing, changeable) social relations and mechanisms of signification.[16]

Theologian Daniel Taylor puts it rather more precisely:

> We belong to communities of belief which help shape, whether we are conscious of it or not, our views of the world and our actions in it. We both draw from these communities and contribute to them, the reflective and the unreflective alike. They help determine what we are.[17]

That is, subcultures are constantly defining and redefining their ideals and aspirations, at the same time seeking out cultural forms and activities that will best allow them to realize those ideals in the form of pleasure. The pleasure thus sought is that of personal gratification within the confines, and with the approval, of a particular subculture, which serves to provide a context for pleasure and to reinforce the validity of such an undertaking, yet with little regard to the larger (moral, social, or cultural) significance or any absolute consequences of such a pursuit. John Frow, quoting Fiske, observes, "'The viewer makes meaning and pleasures from [the text] that are relevant to his or her social allegiance at the moment of viewing; the criteria for relevance *precede* the viewing moment.'"[18]

In this respect, popular culture does not differ from any of the other cultural expressions and contexts of a society. They all exist and are sustained by the pursuit of pleasure. We will examine the relationship between culture, cultures, and popular culture in chapter 1, before going on to consider the particular calling of the evangelical subculture in chapter 2 and the sources of popular culture in chapter 3. The primary concern with popular culture is twofold. First, it is the largest, most all-embracing form of culture—while also the most variegated—in our society. Second, it promotes the self as the ultimate locus of decision-making and authority regarding what is or should be pleasurable. As we shall see, given the inherently sinful nature of the self, such an agenda can lead, on the one hand, to personal disillusionment and social disarray (the futility of popular culture as a primary subculture) and, on the other hand, to the destruction of all meaning (the absurdity of popular culture).

For the evangelical Christian to reap the benefits of popular culture without becoming overwhelmed by it—as it were, to control the kudzu of popular culture—he or she must have standards that facilitate getting beyond the mere self to a more fixed and reliable realm of the experience of pleasure. As Ken Myers writes, "As Christians, we insist that there *are* permanent standards for culture."[19] For the evangelical, these standards must come from God, who enables people to know pleasure and encourages them to do so to the extent that their pleasure corresponds in increasing measure to His own. What these standards are, and how evangelicals may employ them in a kingdom approach to popular culture, will be considered in chapter 4. Those standards, applied within the context of the distinctive calling of the evangelical subculture, together with the various approaches to popular culture we have outlined above, can help to provide an effective evangelical and kingdom approach to popular culture. We will examine this approach in detail in chapter 5.

Finally, in chapter 6 we will set forth some expectations of what evangelicals should hope to gain through a kingdom approach to popular culture. Is it legitimate for evangelical Christians to find pleasure in popular culture? How can we benefit from engaging the popular culture from a kingdom perspective? How will the cause of Christ's kingdom be served? Given that evangelicals are called to seek first the kingdom of God and His righteousness,[20] these are questions to which they must give serious consideration before making any attempt to engage popular culture for the evangelical cause.

Every evangelical is inescapably involved with popular culture. Indeed, for at least some of them, popular culture provides the cultural context and forms *par excellence* for carrying out their callings in Christ. But unless they know what to expect from their involvement in popular culture, and are prepared to engage it with a full-orbed kingdom approach, evangelicals run the risk of being overwhelmed by it, "kudzued" into conformity with the rest of the population. In this case, they will have compromised their callings as citizens of the kingdom of God, abandoned their distinctives as the followers of Christ, and become absorbed into the miasma of self that is the dominant feature of postmodern society.

In undertaking this work, I am especially appreciative of the efforts of three people or groups of people. First is Ken Myers, whose work, *All God's Children and Blue Suede Shoes,* remains the starting point for any study of popular culture from an evangelical perspective. In his ministry with *Mars Hill Journal,* Ken is rendering a valuable service by teaching the evangelical church how to think about all cultural forms, not just popular culture, in order to take every thought captive and make it obedient to Jesus Christ. I am also grateful for the work of Dan Allender and the staff of *Mars Hill Review* (not related to Ken Myers's work, but complementary to it). This feisty, thoughtful, and thoroughly biblical journal is an excellent source of insight and guidance for understanding, appreciating, and making the most of the opportunities that popular culture provides for those who seek to follow Jesus Christ day by day. The third is my son Casey, who, more than anyone in our family, understands both the allure and the shallowness of much popular (and contemporary Christian) culture, and is set on a course of taming this unruly vine for the service of Christ. His work has already resulted in two ambitious CDs of what I would call avant-garde prophetic Christian music, as well as numerous thoughtful works in pen and ink, and he continues to challenge my own thinking about popular culture and how it relates to the work of Christ's kingdom.

I am also grateful to Allan Fisher of P&R Publishing Company for his encouragement and assistance in this project, and to my wife Susie, without whose prayers, support, and keen insights none of my written works would ever get out of the starting gate.

Like kudzu, popular culture just keeps on growing. It may be lovely to look at, and it may well serve some very important purposes in our society. But it can easily get out of control and threaten to overwhelm and "kudzu-ize" all other forms and expressions of culture. It is my conviction that this would not be a good thing. And it is the burden of this book to help equip and encourage the followers of Christ to fight the good fight, not just in controlling the kudzu, but in furthering the kingdom of Christ and His glory.

One

Culture, Cultures, and Popular Culture

Every culture has at its core a view of life and the world that is fundamentally religious and that is expressed in social order as well as sacred practices. Yet no culture joins all its customs and social wisdom in one harmonious whole. Further, it is precisely at the heart of a culture that rebellion from God will be most evident.
—Edmund Clowney[1]

Woe is me, that I sojourn in Mesech, that I dwell in the tents of Kedar!
—Psalm 120:5

Culture is an inescapable feature of human life. Made in the image of the Creator God, people are designed to be makers and users of things, promulgators of laws, developers of languages, creators of institutions, and bearers of traditions. "To be human," writes William D. Romanowski, "is to be created in God's image as an inherently cultural being."[2] There has never been a society of human beings, be it ever so primitive and unsophisticated, without culture. And there seems to be no end to the diversity of ways that people find to express themselves through culture.

Jacques Barzun defines culture as "the traditional things of mind and spirit, the interests and abilities acquired by taking thought; in short, the effort that used to be called cultivation—cultivation of the self."[3] John Storey is rather more concise and down-to-earth, defining culture as "the texts and practices of everyday life."[4] Ken Myers gets even more to the point when he describes culture as

> a dynamic pattern, an ever-changing matrix of objects, artifacts, sounds, institutions, philosophies, fashions, enthusiasms, myths, prejudices, relationships, attitudes, tastes, rituals, habits, colors, and loves, all embodied in individual people, in groups and collectives and associations of people (many of whom do not know they are associated), in books, in buildings, in the use of time and space, in wars, in jokes, and in food.[5]

For a rather more practical definition, we might say that culture consists of the collection of artifacts, institutions, and conventions by which people define, sustain, and enrich themselves.

Culture is inevitable; indeed, it is an inescapable and essential feature of human life. As I am writing these words, I am completely immersed in a wide range of cultural artifacts, institutions, and conventions. The music on my CD player; the Wyeth prints on my walls; all the books on my shelves, as well as the shelves themselves; my lamp, computer, printer, and the paper in it; the carpet on my floor and the clothes on my back: these are just a few of the artifacts of culture that help to define, sustain, and enrich my life. I am using a traditional keyboard to type these words, following a tried-and-true method of typing (convention) that has served many generations in our culture, and using a language (institution) that hundreds of millions of my contemporaries share. I am following the guidelines (convention) of my publisher (institution) so that my manuscript (artifact) will be acceptable for publication (convention). Later today I will cut my grass, using yet more artifacts of contemporary Western culture and following a venerable American convention: keeping one's yard neat and tidy.

Culture is all around us. We live it, eat and drink it, wear it, share it, rely on it, and pass it on to others. To be human is to be a creature of culture. And culture is extremely important since it "helps constitute the structure and shape the history."

> In other words, cultural texts, for example, do not simply reflect history, they make history and are part of its processes and practices and should, therefore, be studied for the (ideological) work that they do, rather than for the (ideological) work (always happening elsewhere) that they reflect.[6]

Yet this cultural involvement in which we are inescapably enmeshed can be extremely complex, even confusing. This is especially true for Americans. It can be difficult to know what is required of us, what is available to us, or what we should do with any of the various cultural forms that confront us at any time. It can be especially difficult when we find ourselves in a new or unfamiliar cultural context, when that context is disagreeable or unpleasant for us, or when it is fraught with ambiguity and uncertainty.

For example, when we first moved to West Virginia from Baltimore, I went to a local grocery store to buy some things. When I reached the cash register, I realized that all I had to pay for my food was a check. Where we had come from, one could not cash a check without first acquiring a check-cashing card from the store. So I asked the girl who waited on me, "Do I need a check-cashing card to be able to use a check?" She looked up, smiled, and said cheerily, "Naw, we'll larn ya." Here was a convention—of neighborly trust and goodwill—that I had rarely seen when living near a large eastern city. I was at first a little taken aback; then I was filled with a sense of delight at the prospect of being part of such a community.

On an earlier occasion, I was attending a rock concert in a large basement hall. On stage, the guitarist was wailing away, the drummer was pounding madly on his skins, and the bass player was thumping wildly at his frets, while they all sang at the top of their lungs some indecipherable lyrics about who knows what. I was in the back, watching the audience. Since there were no chairs in the hall, with only some cushions and large beanbags scattered about, the floor was wide open for dancing. However, only a handful of young people made any movements at all. The crowd mostly stood by watching, talking, looking around, and occasionally clapping. They seemed not quite sure what exactly to do in this situation. The situation would have been much less ambiguous, I'm sure, if this rock concert was not being held in the basement of a church. Convention tells us that we do not dance in church; but then, convention tells us as well that it is highly unusual to have a rock concert in a church. Should we even be here? And what may we do, now that we are here, apparently with the approval of the church authorities?

American Cultures

All of this is simply to illustrate that, in many ways, in America especially, we live in a time not only of varied cultures, but of changing cultures, as well as of clashing or intersecting cultures. This can make it very confusing and even a little disconcerting at times to know exactly how we are to conduct ourselves in particular situations.

This is perhaps because of the unique cultural context of American society, where a common culture, various specific subcultures, and a widespread popular culture intersect, overlap, and intrude on one another. All Americans live in more than one of these cultural settings simultaneously—in most cases, in many of them. Moreover, the growing popular culture intersects with all other cultures in a way that threatens to supplant them all, even to the point of replacing the common culture, or, at least, of causing the culture as a whole to submit to its forms and distinctives. This explains the outcries against the popular culture that come from so many different quarters. People in the various cultures and subcultures of our society are be-

FIGURE 1.1.
COMMON CULTURE

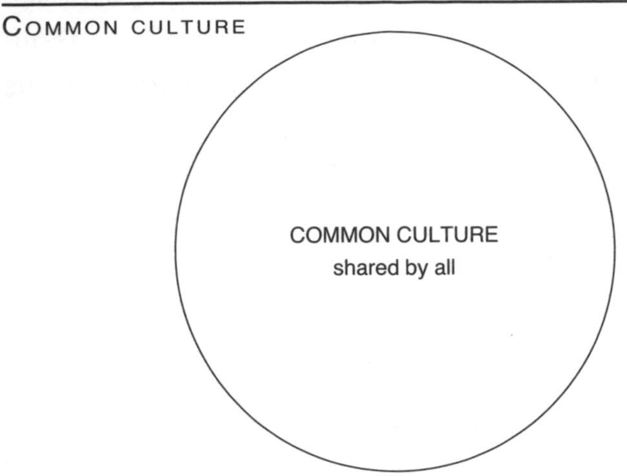

ginning to realize that they are in danger of being overgrown by the kudzu of Mesech and Kedar, and this is true for evangelical Christian culture as well.

Let me see if I can illustrate this. Figure 1.1 represents the *common culture* in which all Americans share by virtue of their living in this society. If you live in America, you are involved in the American common culture. Our American common culture consists of artifacts, institutions, and conventions that are available to, and enjoyed by, all Americans. These include such artifacts as telephones, televisions, and kitchen appliances, such institutions as the democratic process and formal education, and such conventions as driving on the right side of the road and celebrating the Fourth of July. Such cultural forms can be found virtually anywhere one goes in American society. They are part of the common culture of all Americans.

In addition to the common culture, American society

is characterized by a wide range of specific *subcultures.* Some of these are ethnic: Asian, Latin-American, African-American, Amish, etc. Others are local or regional: Appalachian culture, the cultural interests and activities of people in the western suburbs of Philadelphia, inner-city culture, and so forth. Still other subcultures are institutional: the protocols and policies we submit to in our work (corporate culture), the rituals and camaraderie of a sports league, the requirements of a profession, the rites of a fraternity or service club. And still other subcultures are religious: Orthodox Jewish, evangelical Christian, Roman Catholic, Muslim, etc.—each having its own distinctive diversions, activities, holy days, ethic, and so on. Then there is a subculture that is often referred to as "high" culture—primarily by those involved in it—which involves such things as the opera, the theater, or a symphony orchestra.

All these specific subcultures—regimes of value or communities of belief—interact in various ways, mainly because very few Americans live their lives entirely in one or the other of them. Rather, we travel between them at the same time that we share together in the common culture. And as a result of this traffic, a certain amount of "borrowing" and "cross-pollinating" necessarily occurs. Yet most Americans find their individual identity primarily within one or another of the subcultural groups of which they are a part, as we have seen. Thus, these subcultures play very important roles in American life. We might illustrate this aspect of American culture as in figure 1.2.

FIGURE 1.2.

COMMON CULTURE AND SPECIFIC SUBCULTURES

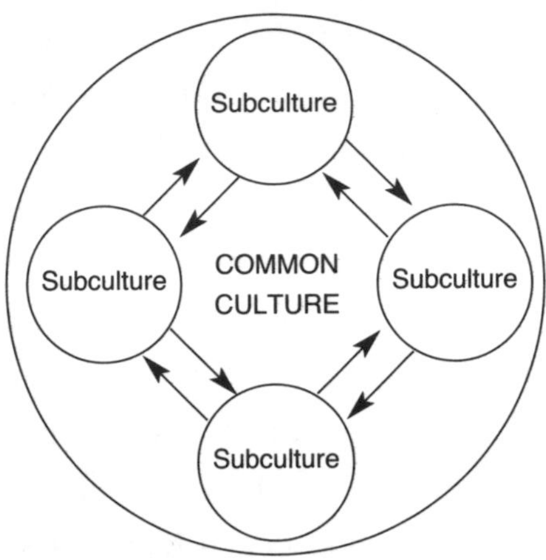

Finally, American society houses a large and diverse *popular culture,* which cuts across, borrows freely from, intersects with, and intrudes upon all other cultural spheres, and is ever growing and expanding, threatening to overwhelm individual subcultures and to replace a large portion of the common culture with itself. We might illustrate the popular culture as in figure 1.3.

FIGURE 1.3.

POPULAR CULTURE

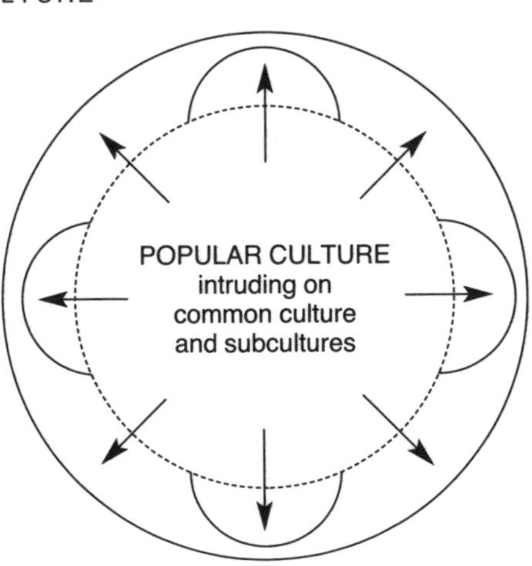

Popular culture includes a wide range of forms, technologies, activities, and outlets. It appeals strongly to individual ideas of pleasure and gratification, promoting a pluralistic view of values and truth. Popular culture has a greater reach into American society than any of the specific subcultural groups. We need to look more closely at this popular culture, which threatens to overshadow and overwhelm all other cultural spheres in our society. What are its characteristics, and what threat does it pose to the evangelical community?

Characteristics of Popular Culture

We may identify six primary characteristics of popular culture.

Popularity. Pop culture has mass appeal. As Romanowski has observed, "Popular artworks are intended to reach mass audiences that cross national, class, religious, political, ethnic, racial, and gender boundaries."[7] Popular culture offers something for everyone. It originates from within all the various cultural spheres, adopts forms and modes of expression that are common to all of them, and appeals to people in every subculture, regardless of their ethnic background, interests, upbringing, social status, or level of education. Look at the people at a baseball game, rock concert, or film. They come from different ethnic and socioeconomic groups. But here they are, in the common pursuit of pleasure, actively participating in the popular culture. Elements of popular culture can be found in the homes of people from virtually every ethnic or religious background. Popular cultural events and activities draw together a wide variety of people who, but for their common participation in popular culture, might otherwise never be involved with one another.

No segment of our society is free from the presence and effects of popular culture; its artifacts, institutions, and conventions penetrate to every cultural sphere in American society. As Thomas S. Hibbs has observed, "No one can escape its influence."[8] Indeed, it is for this very reason that we refer to this expression of American cultural life as *popular*.

Diversity. Popular culture is incredibly diverse. It includes everything from television and pop music to film, romance literature, video games, fashion, sports, and more besides, as well as all the technologies and media by which these various expressions of popular culture carve out their niche. Popular culture

> ranges from home movies to access television to studio-produced programming; from spiritualist groups to trade union seminars; from home gardening to pornography; from beach cricket to organized professional football; and from heavy metal to the Reader's Digest.[9]

Not everyone gravitates to every form of popular culture; however, in at least some forms it manages to confront all of us. We may not listen to pop music, but we like professional sports or enjoy a quiet evening at home with the television. One way or another, we will have our popular culture–or it will have us–and it seems almost to anticipate our every wish and whim by its many and diverse new offerings year after year.

Entertainment. Popular culture is entertainment oriented. It thrives on providing short-term enjoyment. We can see this in three ways. First of all, we see it in its focus on the emotions more than the intellect. Although it does not bypass or ignore the intellect, popular culture intends to make the intellect subservient to the emotions and often leads to rationalizations for indulgence based more on feeling than reason, and an exaltation of experience over thought.[10]

A second way in which the entertainment orientation of popular culture appears is in its commitment more to delight and divert than to educate and edify. The motto of popular culture might be summarized by the slogan so often heard during the 1960s comedy show *Laugh-In,* "If it feels good, do it." The success of any aspect of popular culture is measured by its ability to bring pleasure to the largest number of people. Again, this experience of pleasure is neither evil nor decadent in and of itself. Nor is it devoid of educational or edifying effects; rather, and this has been one of the concerns so often expressed about popular culture, the nature of its educational power is often considered to be more destructive than constructive, both for the individual and for society as a whole. As Ken Myers observes, "The erosion of character, the spoiling of innocent pleasures, and the cheapening of life itself that often accompany modern popular culture can occur so subtly that we believe nothing has happened."[11]

As a result, popular culture, in its effort to entertain, is driven more by concerns of the market than by aesthetics. The question determining the value of any form of popular culture is not Is it beautiful? or Is it good? or Is it true? but Will it sell? Questions of beauty, truth, and morality are certainly involved, but they are strictly secondary. Popular culture is dominated by a concern for the bottom line.[12]

Instability. Popular culture is inherently unstable. It has an ephemeral quality that breeds a mentality of "stars," "hits," and trends, and it results in little of lasting value. As tastes change, forms evolve, new artists appear, and new vehicles for the distribution of popular culture emerge. Familiar artifacts, institutions, and conventions fade away and are replaced by new, albeit equally tentative, ones.[13] At the same time, those new forms partake of the same basic characteristics of popular culture and are thus susceptible to obsolescence and replacement in turn.

Interconnectedness. Popular culture is interconnected, so that its various forms tend to intertwine their tendrils and cultivate links between and among themselves, each one drawing on the entertainment value of the others to strengthen its own position in the marketplace.[14] Go to a professional sporting event, for example, and you will be treated to blaring rock music, high-tech instant replays, and a plethora of opportunities to improve your personal *couture* with all manner of items of sports fashion. The same can be said of any of the forms of popular culture. Like certain microorganisms brought together in a petri dish, the various forms of popular culture tend to interact readily and to promote each other.

Expansiveness. Popular culture is expansionist, ever seeking to establish new beachheads, conquer new territory, create new markets, and realize a bigger bottom line. It is the role of the media, technology, advertising, credit cards, shopping malls, and, increasingly, the Internet—decidedly popular forms of culture—to ensure that popular culture continues to expand into new territory for its market-driven enterprise. If American society as a whole is the open field in which popular culture is sown, then the media, technology, advertising, credit cards, malls, and the Internet are the light, water, and fertilizer by which this cultural kudzu takes root and spreads.

Given these characteristics—popularity, diversity, entertainment, instability, interconnectedness, and expansionism—it is easy to see why popular culture has established such a broad base, and why it threatens to overshadow and overwhelm other expressions of culture in American society. Without a clear understanding of popular culture and an effective approach to dealing with it, those for whom a specific subculture provides their primary context of identity and significance—such as evangelical Christians—risk losing their cultural distinctiveness. They can be absorbed or overwhelmed by cultural forms and expressions that might actually undermine their identity and role within the larger common culture.

Two Examples

Let's take a look at two specific examples of popular culture in order to see, first, how they illustrate the characteristics summarized above and, second, how they pose a threat to evangelical distinctiveness in America.

Pop music. Pop music is not a distinctively modern phenomenon. There have always been musical forms in the cultures of the world that appealed to people because of their simplicity, affective power, or everyday or risqué themes. However, never has there been such a proliferation of songs, artists, and outlets for pop music, never have so many people availed themselves of pop music so intensely or with so much consistency, and never has such a large slice of a nation's economy been represented by this cultural form.

Pop music is ubiquitous and brings its cultural forms to bear on Americans from a great many angles. I may not listen to the local pop radio station, but if I go out to eat, watch TV, attend a sporting event, or hear any advertising on the radio, pop music will find its way to my ears.

At the same time, pop music is ephemeral. Pop stars come and go as the entertainment-hungry audience for pop music moves on to graze in new fields. Pop charts change daily as they measure the emotional response of listeners and the market viability of a particular disc or artist. Pop singers and musicians who commanded large and adoring audiences in a previous generation are all but unknown by the contemporary pop audience. Few of the pop music "hits" of previous generations have any standing whatsoever with contemporary listeners. (Recently my daughter Ashley was playing the *White Album* in her car, when a fellow college student asked her what it was, saying he had never heard of it.)

And the pop music industry continues to grow. Each passing year brings new artists, new albums, new distributors, more concerts, and greater financial success.

Moreover, pop music's success has affected various subcultures of American society at the same time that it has intruded into virtually every area of life. Symphony orchestras, in order to capitalize on the success of pop music, sponsor "pops" concerts, in which pop music "classics" are adapted for orchestral performance to the delight of "high culture" customers. Ethnic and regional music groups adapt their traditional music to pop instruments and rhythms. Private headsets isolate us in a world of pop music diversion on a plane, while jogging or working out, or simply while walking to work. Like rats at a Skinner bar, we mash the rewind button over and over to reward our affections with uninterrupted pleasure. We can't even get away from pop music on the telephone, where we are assaulted by its rhythms, melodies, and lyrics while we wait on hold for our call to be completed. (Think of the wonderful commercial featuring a man whose car has broken down in the desert, who asks the repair shop to keep him on hold so that he can finish dancing to a particularly enjoyable pop tune.)

The cultural kudzu of pop music has taken root in every nook and cranny of American society, and its shadow can be seen to be growing over increasingly large areas of life. This is not all bad, as I will argue in more detail in a later chapter, since there is a certain inherent beauty and utility to popular music. At the same time, pop music threatens to overwhelm whole sectors of the common culture and specific subcultures of our society.

We can see something of this in the effect of pop music on worship in the evangelical community. In many respects, the "worship wars" currently raging within that community have to do with whether or not pop music forms, technologies, and melodies are appropriate for corporate worship. In many churches, the tendrils of pop music have altogether replaced such traditional liturgical accoutrement as choirs, organs, and hymns. Claiming that pop music is what our contemporaries know and will resonate to, supporters of innovation urge the replacement of traditional liturgical forms with those of popular culture, saving only the lyrics of traditional music as testimony to the distinctiveness of worship. This frequently leaves traditional worshipers upset and in a quandary, not quite sure how to react or what to do as their church begins to look more and more like the world around them. And a burgeoning Christian pop music industry virtually guarantees that the rising generation of evangelicals will increasingly gravitate to pop forms as their primary source of musical inspiration and enjoyment.

This is not the place to debate the merits of using the forms of contemporary popular music in a liturgical context. My only point is to show how, from the perspective of many in the evangelical community, it might be seen that worship is being overgrown by the kudzu of rock music and is losing its distinctiveness.

Sports. As a second example, consider the popular culture form of sports. Again, people in every age have had their games and diversions, but only in the last generation or two has the craze for sports taken on the character of kudzu. The combination of television, advertising, and the high visibility of sports stars has made participation in sports, as either player or fan, a virtual *sine qua non* of American life. Parents sign up their children for soccer, football, or lacrosse in the fall, basketball or volleyball (or indoor soccer) in the winter, and baseball or softball in the spring and summer. Tennis and golf camps for children are on the rise. Enormous amounts of money are spent, and even larger quantities of time are invested, in equipment, uniforms, camps, practice sessions, games, and celebrations. Children grow up thinking that sports are as much a part of American life as going to school—and, for many, more important than going to church. Many, especially those recognized as particularly gifted, devote themselves to earning college scholarships or making it to the pros, sacrificing other interests and activities along the way. Meanwhile, the ambiance of their homes is continuously awash in sports programming, brought in not only by the major TV networks, but by cable channels devoted to nothing but sports, as well as a proliferation of sports magazines.

The hype, celebrity, and excitement of the sports environment are part of a steady diet in many American homes. Significant portions of the wardrobe of both children and adults reflect a fascination with sports: jerseys, caps, shoes, and designer wear for all ages. Adults continue playing sports well into their senior years, showing that the impression made on them as children certainly took hold. And the success of the sports industry induces other sectors of American life—advertising, charitable giving, education, and politics, among others—to draw on sports figures and themes to enhance their own visibility and success.

Sports can be a valuable asset in the life of the church, as the development of sports ministries over the past twenty years has shown (and as we shall see later). However, in many ways sports have begun to overwhelm the culture of the evangelical community, especially in the observance of the Lord's Day and the availability of children and adults for involvement in church activities. For some time, I was a pastor in a community in South Florida, and it never failed, on those Sundays when the Miami Dolphins were playing at home, that members of the congregation would leave worship before the service was over so that they could get to the stadium on time. (I have already been advised in my current ministry not to sponsor any training activities on Saturdays in the fall when the Tennessee Vols are in town.) Uncountable numbers of evangelicals think nothing of spending their Sunday afternoons either playing sports, attending a sporting event, or watching one on television—practices that previous generations of evangelicals would have considered unthinkable.

Some churches allow their softball teams to play games on Sunday morning, during the time when the rest of the congregation is at worship, and will conduct a special early service just for the team. Parents allow their children to play on "traveling teams," many of which hold their games on Sundays, and feel no compunction whatsoever about the whole family missing church on those days.

Youth and children's workers moan about how difficult it is to conduct effective ministries during the week, when they have to compete with sports programs at school and in the community. Adults, weary with work and with running their children here and there to practices and games, have little strength left for ministry activities or leadership in local churches. Many churches will cancel or reschedule their Sunday evening service on Super Bowl Sunday, since they know that a good many of their members will choose to stay at home rather than come to worship. Or they may even devote the evening service to watching the game together, as a special "outreach" or "fellowship" event.

The culture of sports has penetrated the life of the evangelical community, threatening the sanctity of the day of rest, inhibiting the church's ability to equip and send its members for ministry, and undermining other aspects of its distinctiveness as a subculture in American society. Yet, for the most part, evangelicals seem hardly troubled by this—certainly not as much as many of them are about the presence of pop music in the church. The evangelical community is in danger of being overgrown by the kudzu of sports, and is so enamored of the beauty and virility of this intruder that it does not sense the threat to its distinctiveness as a community.

A Caveat and a Challenge

All that has been said must not be taken as a ringing condemnation of pop music or sports, much less of popular culture as a whole. That has not been the intent. Popular culture has much to commend it; as Graham Cray puts it, popular culture "can have its moments of transcendence."[15] In addition, there is even much that evangelicals can learn from popular culture about fulfilling their own distinctive calling. My purpose is not to sound the alarm regarding popular culture. Instead, it is to explain something of the character of this uniquely modern and postmodern phenomenon so as to alert evangelicals to the inherent dangers of an unguarded approach to popular culture, and to highlight the need to equip them to deal with it. Evangelicals can learn to appreciate the beauty of this cultural kudzu and gain the benefit it has to offer, without allowing it to overgrow everything that makes them who they are.

Popular culture is neither evil nor decadent *per se.* Rather, popular culture is inevitable. The challenge to evangelicals is to recognize the futility of popular culture as a primary cultural context for life and to reject its absurdities, in order to arrest its decaying effects on their own distinctive calling in American society. As Jacques Barzun has observed, "When people accept futility and the absurd as normal, the culture is decadent."[16] Some may argue that American culture has entered a period of decadence, largely brought on by the success of popular culture.[17] While I may agree with such an assessment, it is not the purpose of this book to argue that point. My object lies elsewhere. The challenge to evangelicals is to keep popular culture from debasing their subculture into a state of decadence, and to equip themselves from within their culture to leaven the rest of society—decadent or not—with the beauty, truth, and glory of God as these are expressed in the artifacts, conventions, and institutions of a distinctively evangelical subculture. In order to rise to this twofold challenge, evangelicals will first need to make sure that they understand their own distinctive calling in life. Then they may begin to equip and discipline themselves to appreciate and participate in popular culture in such a way as to benefit from its beauty and resist its undermining power. Understanding our mission as a kingdom people will allow us to consider a kingdom approach to popular culture, so that, controlling this kudzu, we might gain its benefit without being overwhelmed by it.

Study Questions

1. In which of the various subcultures of our society do you find yourself a participant? How has popular culture intruded into those subcultures?
2. With which of the various forms of popular culture—for example, music, film, television programming—are you most familiar? How would you characterize your involvement in these various forms (think back

to the approaches to popular culture outlined in the introduction)? What benefits do you gain from your involvement with these cultural forms?

3. Do you agree with the author that there is a danger that certain forms of popular culture may begin to "overgrow" the distinctive culture of the evangelical Christian community? Why or why not?
4. Do any aspects of contemporary popular culture trouble you? In what ways? Has popular culture contributed to decadence in our society?
5. What goals would you like to set for this study? How do you hope to grow in your ability to understand and use popular culture? How would you like to see your involvement with popular culture improved or changed as a result of this study?

Two

Popular Culture and Our Kingdom Calling

To advance Christ's kingdom defines the Christian's life.
—EDMUND CLOWNEY[1]

But seek ye first the kingdom of God, and his righteousness.
—MATTHEW 6:33

Amid the various cultures and subcultures of the world, an all-embracing, all-transcending reality has been established which—even more than popular culture—cuts across, infiltrates, pervades, and will ultimately overwhelm and supplant all others. This is the presence—and the culture—of the kingdom of God.

For some readers, it may seem strange to talk about a "culture" of the kingdom of God. After all, is not the kingdom of God "not of this world"?[2] Does it not emphasize righteousness, peace, and joy in the Spirit over against such mundane things as eating and drinking and other forms of culture?[3] Is not its power concerned above all else with spiritual realities?[4] How then can we speak of the kingdom of God as though it were also to be involved with music, literature, everyday diversions, fleeting fashions, and the various ways in which we seek to entertain, recreate, and amuse ourselves? Are not these things rather to be avoided than indulged? Surely to drag the heavenly kingdom into such matters is to debase and devalue it. Are we not better advised to seek the virtues and benefits of Christ's kingdom apart from all such concerns, to "come out from among them . . . and touch not the unclean thing," as it were?[5]

For two reasons, this is quite impossible. First, popular culture is constantly growing and expanding, extending its tendrils and pressing in on us from all sides, even though we have been set apart for a kingdom calling in Jesus Christ. We could not avoid popular culture if we tried. Second, and more important, it is the very nature of our kingdom calling to interact with the world. While it is true that we have been set apart for God and are not to love the world or the things in it,[6] we still exist *in* the world and have been charged with a mission in that world of reconciling all things to God.[7] All things in the world have been put under the authority of Christ the King, and He has commissioned us to plunder the holdings of His adversary, who has laid hold of popular culture and is using it for his own demonic ends.[8] God has given all things into our hands as His servants.[9] And He calls us to take captive everything that exalts itself against Him and make it obedient to Christ.[10] We are to exercise dominion over the world and everything in it.[11] Everything we do is to be done for God's glory and honor,[12] and this presumably includes our involvement with popular culture.

Thus, we may not pick and choose among the things of this world, selecting only certain ones of them to address or engage as Christians. Everything that comes across our path must be taken in hand, made subject to His rule, refashioned and reprogrammed, and put to work in advancing His kingdom. As Edmund Clowney puts it, "The Christian struggles to overcome the disorder of sin and to preserve and develop God's world. . . . The church of Christ builds a spiritual culture, a foretaste of the kingdom to come."[13] The world and everything in it belong to God.[14] Therefore, whatever we encounter in the world is a legitimate target for our kingdom calling of reconciling all things to Him. Since popular culture is unavoidable, we will certainly encounter it in the course of our kingdom service. Therefore, we may neither ignore nor avoid popular culture; nor may we merely indulge ourselves in it in the same way that our unsaved friends and neighbors do, lest we be overwhelmed by the kudzu of popular culture, just as they are. Rather, we must be prepared to understand, seize, and enlist popular culture for the cause of Christ our King.

But for us to do this consistently—as we shall see more fully in subsequent chapters—we must first make certain that we understand the nature of our kingdom calling in Christ. Only then will we be able to see more clearly why that calling requires us to address, engage, and take captive the popular culture of our day for the purposes of Christ and His kingdom.

The Kingdom of God

The kingdom of God is not a place, but a *dominion.* It is, according to Herman Ridderbos, "pre-eminently the idea of the kingly self-assertion of God, of his coming to the world in order to reveal his royal majesty, power and right."[15] Clowney writes, "In the Scriptures, God's kingdom is the shadow of his presence; not so much his domain as his dominion; not his realm but his rule. God's kingdom is the working of his power to accomplish his purposes of judgment and salvation."[16] The kingdom of God is the presence of God Himself, working through His Word and Spirit to accomplish His eternal redemptive purposes on earth. While the kingdom orbits around and pervades the church as the community of the redeemed, it nonetheless is present throughout the world as the Spirit of God confronts and woos the people of the earth with their need for God.[17]

Jesus announced that His coming brought that kingdom near—"at hand"—to bear on the hearts of men and women. The kingdom will not be fully realized until the new heavens and the new earth are established, but it is even now advancing on the earth through the ministry of His Spirit.[18] Those who have come to faith in Jesus Christ are called to live within and according to His dominion—His kingdom—during their days on the earth. Five aspects of our calling in the kingdom of Christ can especially help us to understand the inevitability of our being involved with the kudzu of popular culture and, therefore, the importance of our controlling its effects. These are the spiritual nature of our calling, the temporal and material mandate it entails, the manner in which that calling is uniquely fitted to each individual Christian, the communal nature of our kingdom calling, and the eschatological dimension of the kingdom. We shall look at each of these in turn.

The Spiritual Nature of Our Kingdom Calling

We are right to see that the kingdom of God is not of this world, that is, that it is essentially spiritual, which makes it entirely unlike the political kingdoms of men. The kingdom of God is built with spiritual resources. It pursues a spiritual agenda and builds on spiritual foundations. It subordinates all temporal and material concerns to the greater and lasting good of spiritual advancement. And it emphasizes values and priorities that are in many cases antithetical, even hostile, to the values and priorities of those who yet resist the authority of Christ and His kingdom.

The kingdom of God advances according to its unique spiritual character, resources, and agenda, overcoming every obstacle as it grows to fullness according to the wise plan and counsel of God. In the book of Daniel, we see some of the implications of the spiritual nature of the kingdom. Daniel was shown that the kingdom of God is like a growing stone, one not cut by human hands, which, upon impacting the earth, grows and spreads until it overcomes every other kingdom and fills the entire earth.[19] The kingdoms that Nebuchadnezzar saw in his dream were all made by human beings, symbolized by the precious metals on the body of the great image. Each of those kingdoms would be overturned by a successive one, less pure and precious than itself, and this would ultimately result in a world of political instability, represented by the mixed iron and clay of the final empire. But the kingdom that God would send to earth during the years of that last empire would not be made by human hands. Its source would be divine, as its power would be. No human kingdom would be able to stand against it as it advanced irresistibly to realize its full purpose on earth.

However, conflict and interaction with human kingdoms would occur, as we learn in Daniel 7. Daniel was shown that the kingdoms of men would oppose the kingdom of God, even to the extent of persecuting those who are part of it (v. 25). This implies that the people of God's kingdom are different, that there are things about them that, because of their spiritual orientation, provoke their neighbors and the leaders of their communities to strike out at them. They have different values and ethics; they engage in different social and cultural activities; and, we might suppose, they call into question—if only by their distinctive way of life—the practices of those whose lives are different from theirs. The spiritual orientation and priorities of the people in God's kingdom often lead them to be at cross-purposes with those whose agenda and values are of another sort, and who pursue that agenda through the various agencies of culture, including popular culture.

At the same time, the spiritual power into which they have entered enables the people of God to be strong, to undertake many remarkable works, and to lead many to righteousness with them.[20] This implies, among other things, the ability to communicate effectively—to understand the concerns of neighbors, speak intelligently to them, help them to see the errors in their thinking, and show them how they, too, may enter into the new reality of the kingdom of God. The spiritual power that makes God's people different also enables them to do many good works and to bear convincing testimony to the reality of new life in the kingdom of God. As that power—the power of God's Spirit working according to His Word—is expressed in His people, it leads them into all manner of social and cultural activities and environments, where their unique kingdom life and orientation enable them to stand out socially and culturally and to interact with others for the sake of advancing the kingdom.

Thus, the spiritual nature of the kingdom of God finds expression in and through earthly things, including culture. And, given the growth of popular culture, it is inevitable that kingdom culture—the righteousness of God expressed in artifacts, institutions, and conventions—will encounter and engage popular culture across a broad front.

The Kingdom Mandate

The kingdom of God has a mandate to grow and fill the earth with the presence of the divine glory, as we have seen. From the beginning of God's dealings with people, this mandate has had a strong cultural—and therefore temporal—aspect. Adam and Eve were given the duty of exercising dominion over all the earth, beginning in the Garden of Eden.[21] In taking up the calling to cultivate the garden, they became involved in all manner of cultural activities—communicating with one another, naming the animals, tending to the plants and trees, and so forth. The fall into sin did not negate this mandate. We see its restatement to Noah in Genesis 9 and David reflecting on its continuing validity in Psalm 8. The words of Christ in Matthew 5:13–16, that the church is to be salt and light to the world, imply that these all-pervading influences would reach into every realm of culture and society.

We have already mentioned the comprehensive nature of Christ's kingdom rule and of our calling in that kingdom. Our kingdom calling clearly requires that we take up the duty assigned to our first parents and bring the temporal and material realm into subjection to Christ. Beginning with our own lives—our bodies, time, possessions, roles, relationships, responsibilities, and cultural activities—we are charged with laboring to bring out the goodness that God has invested in the many gifts and things that He has given us, so that in all our undertakings He might be glorified. In Scripture we find the saints of God interacting with the culture of their day and drawing it into service for the purposes of God. Solomon's employment of the Gentile Huram-abi[22] and David's use of popular tunes for many of his psalms are examples of the way in which the rule of God interacts with the cultures of the day. Indeed, the many literary genres in which Scripture was given also indicate the potential fruitfulness of cultural interaction for the sake of God's eternal purposes and plan.

Similarly, we must be prepared, in taking up our calling in the kingdom of God, to make use of the many and varied cultural resources and opportunities around us, including those afforded by the popular culture. Our kingdom mandate is not simply to save people's souls. We are called to make disciples, and disciples, being image-bearers of God, are cultural creatures, as we have seen. Thus, our mandate requires that we be prepared to speak to the involvement of Christ's disciples in culture, and to prepare them to engage others of different cultures for the sake of Christ and His kingdom.

The Individuality of the Kingdom

Unlike many of the mass movements of history, the kingdom of God does not require of those who participate in it that they all wear the same uniform, cut their hair in the same manner, or march in lockstep to the same music. The kingdom of God is as varied and individual as the people who have come into its embrace, and it offers plenty of room for all manner of expression of cultural interest.

The mountain of the Lord's house is a mountain with many peaks, as the psalmist reminds us.[23] Each peak has a different altitude and shape, unique faces and slopes, and different flora and fauna. Each peak has its own identity and place in the mountain of the Lord's house. Paul's analogy of the church as members of a human body leads us to the same conclusion.[24] In the kingdom of God, we are wondrously different, and in many ways our differences are what make the kingdom so attractive to those on the outside. We march under a common banner of kingdom principles, but we find no obligatory dress or speech, no uniform employment, and no single way of expressing membership. As William D. Romanowski puts it, "A biblical idea of culture as the mandate to explore and cultivate the possibilities woven into God's creation allows for cultural pluralism, while affirming the existence of a world ordered by God."[25] The Spirit of God works in each individual who enters His dominion to bring kingdom fruit and power to light in virtually unlimited ways.

In the same way, as the people of God's kingdom participate in the culture around them, they do so in ways that identify them as representatives of that heavenly realm. Even down to such mundane cultural matters as cuisine and table manners (eating and drinking, 1 Cor. 10:31), the people of God stand out as concerned to bring honor and glory to Him. And they will do so in ways that are uniquely adapted to their own places, gifts, interests, and callings, in the material and temporal order. No two people will dress alike, prefer the same kind of music, work at the same job, delight in the same cuisine, go to the same movies, or inflect their words in exactly the same way when they speak. But their participation in the kingdom of God, with its heavenly orientation and priorities, will be reflected in all they do as they take of the "all things" their King has given them and put them to work to advance His kingdom, bringing the dominion of Christ increasingly to bear on the realities of culture. We should expect, therefore, that the members of Christ's kingdom will follow their unique interests, abilities, and leadings into a wide array of the forms of popular culture, where they will raise a banner to the Lord and begin to reclaim enemy-held territory for His rule.

The Communal Character of the Kingdom

Although the kingdom of God accepts unlimited individuality, it is not individualistic. "Christianity is not an individual and deeply private experience but a very concrete and practical way of life that is learned, practiced, supported, and empowered in its community."[26] The kingdom of God—the power of His Word and Spirit working in the lives of men and women—creates a new community of like-minded people, devoted to serving God with all their interests and abilities and to complementing one another in the communal project of advancing the cause of Christ. The communal character of the kingdom of God serves this kingdom calling in at least three ways.

As a place for kingdom reorientation. It provides a setting for continuous reorientation to the kingdom calling through corporate worship. In worship, the followers of Christ are reminded of God's greatness and grace, they celebrate His glory together and partake of His sacraments, and they scrutinize and reorient their lives before Him for more effective kingdom living in the world. The worship in which God's kingdom people participate is unlike the various activities that postmodern groups pursue together—raves, discussions, celebrations of all kinds, work, teams, clubs, associations, and so forth. Worship lifts kingdom citizens beyond themselves and their temporal and material context into the spiritual reality of the heavenly kingdom, and invites them to reflect from that vantage point on their daily reality.[27] In worship, we enter into a transcendent experience that puts all temporal and material activity into an infinitely beautiful, spectacularly cosmic, and ultimately true setting. Worship gives the community of God's kingdom people an eternal vantage point from which to renew their hope, nurture their spiritual longing, assess their everyday lives, and rededicate themselves to their individual callings in Christ's kingdom.

As a pool of resources. The communal character of the kingdom of God creates a pool of resources from which to draw for advancing the kingdom in the world. Those resources include the individual gifts of different members—for training, service, witness, cultural activity, and so forth—as well as the material resources—facilities, budgets, material goods—to serve and provide for individual members and reach out to those beyond the community of faith. As the worship of God strengthens commitment to Him, community members grow in self-giving, sacrificial service, mutual encouragement and edification, and devotion to the mission of the kingdom. Such inward growth makes a virtually unlimited pool of resources available for advancing the rule of Christ in local communities and around the world, as the first Christian churches found.[28]

As protection against sin. The communal character of the kingdom provides for all its members a healthy safeguard against falling into sin. The various "one another" passages of the New Testament clearly indicate the role of the community in providing admonition, teaching, correction, and stimulation to good works for the members of it.[29] Members of the kingdom community need not shy away from going forth into the world for fear that they will be overwhelmed by it, so long as they maintain open, active, and vital involvement with the rest of the kingdom community. Reoriented and refreshed in worship, retooled through training and sent in mission, they may serve in the world–and in the midst of its popular culture–with confidence, knowing that their community will help them stay the course of their kingdom calling against all the pressures of the unbelieving environment.

Thus, the communal character of the kingdom of God ensures that its members may interact with the world and its cultures–including popular culture–in a manner that is consistent with their kingdom calling.

The Eschatological Nature of the Kingdom

Finally, the eschatological nature of the kingdom of God makes it possible for the members of that heavenly dominion to engage the cultures of their day with vision and confidence. History is on a course determined by God. It will end with the return of Christ, judgment of the nations, and then, for the citizens of the heavenly kingdom, an eternal life of glory and bliss in the new heavens and the new earth. Knowing where we are headed fills us with hope, confidence, and joy. It also calls us to be constantly preparing ourselves for this new reality in our lives here and now.

The apostle Peter calls the members of Christ's kingdom to look forward eagerly to its full coming and to prepare themselves with lives of holiness, godliness, and righteousness as that day approaches.[30] This charge has many implications, at least some of which relate to our involvement in popular culture. We may not hope to escape popular culture, yet we must not be overwhelmed by it, succumbing to its allure and falling in step with its agenda. That would be to live as though we did not expect the Lord to come in judgment of everything that raises itself up against Him. Instead, knowing that the kingdom is advancing and that its full realization is coming, we labor within the popular culture to bring kingdom principles to bear on it. We reach out to those who are enmeshed in the tendrils of its kudzu and call them to find new power and purpose in the context of Christ's kingdom, as we lay hold of the artifacts, institutions, and conventions of popular culture to redeem and reconcile them to the King of glory.

As Eddie Gibbs has written, "The gospel judges each culture according to its compatibility with the focus, values and goals of the kingdom of God."[31] Living in the kingdom, embracing its character and priorities, and knowing its goals and objectives, we take a *pro*spective approach to culture, envisioning and working for its transformation according to the eschatological kingdom perspective in which we live. We anticipate a day in which all human culture will serve nothing but the purposes of Christ and His glory, and we are preparing for that day even now.

Seeking the Kingdom, Subduing the Culture

The kingdom of God is the context within which we live as members of the body of Christ. Jesus has been exalted to the right hand of the Father, and He is putting all things under His feet.[32] His rule is advancing like a growing stone over all the earth and will continue to do so until He comes in glory to consummate God's redemptive plan and usher in the fullness of His kingdom in the new heavens and the new earth. In the meantime, He calls His followers to seek the kingdom of God and His righteousness as their first priority.[33]

Given that the two great commandments are to love the Lord our God with all our heart, mind, and strength and to love our neighbor as ourselves, how does seeking the kingdom of God intersect with and help to clarify what these mandates require? And how does seeking the kingdom help to prepare us to deal with the popular culture of our day?

To love God is to know and delight in Him and His Word, to seek to please and honor Him, and to serve Him according to His good and perfect will. Thus, since our God has commanded us to seek first His kingdom, we must give our hearts to this endeavor, for out of the heart flow all the other issues of life.[34] The heart is the seat of the affections, which, as we saw in the introduction, are so critical to whatever we choose to do in life. Thus, we must pay careful attention to the state of our hearts with respect to the kingdom of God.

Do we love the kingdom of God with all our hearts? Is it the great desire of our lives to know more of Christ's power at work in us, willing and working for His good pleasure?[35] Do we eagerly long for more time with the Lord, to see more of His glory reflected in our lives, and to speak to others about the joys of knowing and serving Him? These are the kinds of questions that allow us to look into our hearts to determine whether we have fully submitted ourselves to the rule of Christ. If we are spending more time, money, and energy on aspects of popular culture than on seeking the kingdom of God, our hearts may need some retooling. If the prospect of a rock concert, our favorite sitcom, or an afternoon at the ball game excites us more than worshiping God, we have some work to do in preparing our hearts to seek the kingdom of God.

Seeking the kingdom with all our hearts, in obedience to the command of Him who calls us to love Him most of all, means that our affections–our hopes, dreams, aspirations, longings, desires, heart inclinations, enthusiasm, and so forth–must be directed at seeing the rule of Christ advance in our own lives and throughout the world. The prospect of this should thrill and motivate us to seek it earnestly. Commitment to kingdom progress must determine our priorities and organize our time. Devotion to seeking the kingdom must come to define the way we interact with all of life, including popular culture. When we are seeking the kingdom with all our hearts, we allow nothing to supplant our love for God and our desire for His rule to advance. All our interaction with the popular culture of our day is governed by this deep desire to seek the kingdom of God and His righteousness.

In the same way, seeking the kingdom requires the full engagement of our minds, renewed in Christ and resisting conformity to the world.[36] We do not have the luxury of checking our brains at the door as we go out into the world, seeking to advance Christ's kingdom. This must be the case especially as we interact with popular culture.

I recall talking with a young Christian in a church I served not long ago. We were discussing popular music, and he mentioned that John Lennon's song "Imagine" was one of his favorites. He and his friends played and sang it incessantly. I agreed that this song had a most enjoyable and even fetching melody, and I asked what he particularly liked about the song. He told me that the music moved him. The subtle, gentle, almost plaintive melody really reached his soul. Then he said he could "really resonate" with the ideas that Lennon was singing about—peace and love, community and sharing, and so forth.

I asked if he had listened carefully to the lyrics, and he said he thought so. Was there anything about the song that troubled him? Not that he could think of. I asked him, "Given your faith in Christ, how can you play with such unqualified approval and sing with such delight—especially before your unsaved friends—a song that declares its commitment to ridding the world of the very things you believe?" "What do you mean?" he asked in reply. So I asked him to sing through the lyrics for me, which he did. "You didn't hear that?" I asked. "Hear what?" I pointed out to him that in John Lennon's ideal world there would be "nothing to kill or die for, and no religion, too." My young friend rationalized that away by saying that Lennon meant only formal, traditional, rigid religion. "But what would take the place of even that?" I asked. "What do you mean?" I pointed out that John Lennon's desire to be rid of religion was a hopeless fantasy, especially since his own vision was nothing more than a humanistic religion that sounded as though it had its roots in Marxist utopianism. If no religions, be they ever so stuffy and formal, existed to check such a vision, where might it lead? "Wow," he said, "I never thought of that."

This is precisely the problem with too much Christian involvement with popular culture. Because popular culture exists to entertain, we are all too willing to let it do that, listening and participating selectively and never asking ourselves what the intellectual price is that we are paying to get our jollies for a few minutes. What ideas, truths, and spiritual values do we have to sublimate? What lies or half-truths do we allow to lodge in our subconscious mind? And what do we communicate about these ideas, truths, and values to those before whom we either minimize or embrace them?

Seeking the kingdom of God with all our minds means that we give ourselves earnestly to understanding biblical ideas of beauty, goodness, and truth, to deciphering the messages of popular culture, and to discovering the concerns and needs of our kudzu-captive contemporaries. We must become clear and devoted thinkers, who use our minds to guide and shape our hearts, so that we may truly seek the kingdom with all our strength as well.

For each of us, physical strength is lodged in our bodies, distributed proportionately throughout, so that each of the members of our body can do its work. It takes a certain kind of strength to focus the eye, engage the tongue for speech, or move the hands and legs in work. Mental concentration—for study, self-discipline, and so forth—is another kind of physical strength that forces the brain to develop new patterns of thinking. Those who are called to seek the kingdom of God must devote their strength—all of it, all the time—to loving God and loving their neighbors. We must not grow weary in using our strength to do good to others, whether that requires listening to them, talking with them, going somewhere with them, or helping them in some way.[37] At the same time, we must not allow the members of our bodies to dissipate their strength in frivolous, sinful activities.[38] *All* our strength must be committed to seeking the kingdom of Christ, so that, whether our ears, eyes, mouths, hands, or heads are engaged, they are being exercised in a manner designed to advance the kingdom of Christ.

This sounds like a daunting challenge, to say the least. But as we learn to devote our hearts and minds more to seeking the kingdom of God, we will find that our bodies will follow as they are directed from within. So when our eyes, ears, brains, hands, and so forth come into contact with popular culture, they will do so in a manner that is disciplined to serve the advance of Christ's kingdom, for this is what it means to love the Lord and seek His kingdom with all our strength.

First Things First

From this point on, our discussion will turn more directly to popular culture and how we as Christians may so engage it as to gain the benefits it offers without being overwhelmed by it. But since seeking the kingdom of God is our first priority in all things, the discussion of this chapter is crucial to controlling the kudzu around us. We have considered nothing new in these pages. Rather, we have taken a brief tour of the foundations of our lives, those "first things" that must always be in place if we are going to fulfill our calling to advance the kingdom of Christ in the face of the challenges of postmodern society—not the least of which is that of controlling the kudzu of popular culture.

We cannot effectively engage the popular culture of our day without first resolving to seek the kingdom of God and His righteousness as the top priority in all we do. But with such a resolution in place, and our understanding of it and commitment to it growing, we may confidently engage the popular culture and expect to benefit from it without being overwhelmed by it.

Study Questions

1. How has this chapter increased your understanding of the kingdom of God? Would you say that seeking that kingdom is the top priority of your life at this time? What makes you say that?
2. In what ways are you actively involved in seeking the kingdom of God? How is the reality of God's kingdom affecting your life? In what ways would you like to see more evidence of the kingdom's presence in your roles, relationships, and responsibilities?
3. How might you expect to see your involvement in popular culture affected by daily renewing your resolve to

seek first the kingdom of God and His righteousness? Does the prospect of this excite or dismay you?

4. Consider the communal character of the kingdom—our worship, sharing in resources, and mutual accountability. How is your involvement in popular culture affected by these? How can you see that these afford rich resources for taking more of a kingdom approach to popular culture?
5. Should Christians expect their commitment to the kingdom of God to eventuate in a distinctively Christian popular culture? Do you see any evidence that this is happening? How might such a culture differ from the popular culture of our postmodern society?

Three

Sources of Popular Culture

All the notable endowments that manifest themselves among unbelievers are gifts of God.
—JOHN CALVIN[1]

Thou hast ascended on high, thou hast led captivity captive: thou hast received gifts for men; yea, for the rebellious also, that the LORD *God might dwell among them.*
—PSALM 68:18

I confess to being mystified from time to time by certain of the forms of popular culture that I encounter. A television series will strike me as so mindless, inane, and altogether devoid of good taste; a rock song may be so cacophonous and lacking in form or sense; an advertisement will be so ludicrous or offensive, or a film so violent, that I find myself asking, Where does this stuff come from? or, How did they manage to come up with that?

Examining the sources of popular culture is a first step in our beginning to understand, appreciate, and control it, allowing us to gain the benefits of popular culture without being overwhelmed by it. The various forms and expressions of popular culture do not spring forth out of nothing. Rather, they originate in sources that we in the evangelical community have in common with those outside the pale of faith who produce the popular culture with which we must contend. When we see the connections between popular culture and the sources from which it derives, we are in a better position to assess, participate in, and appreciate popular culture, and to employ it in our kingdom calling.

For our purposes, we may identify five sources of popular culture: the image of God, the gifts of God, an individual's training and environment, the corrupting effects of sin, and the sovereign moving of God's Spirit. Each of these plays a role in the creation of the artifacts, institutions, and conventions that make up the popular culture of our day. We will examine each of these in turn.

The Image of God

All cultural activity on the part of human beings has its origin ultimately in the image of God, as we have seen. Since people are made in the image of the Creator, they create things as well.

For the purposes of His glory, and according to the intentions of His goodness, God made the heavens and the earth and all things in them, bringing abundant and varied material resources and things into being out of nothing. Like a potter at his wheel, God worked to shape and order these resources until they arrived at a condition of goodness in His eyes. As the crowning achievement of His creation, He made man and woman in His image, after His likeness, and gave them dominion over all the creation.[2] Calvin locates the image of God in the soul, that aspect of our humanity that enables people to know and love God. This is a capacity which no other creature shares.[3] Of the soul Calvin writes:

> Although properly it is not spatially limited, still, set in the body, it dwells there as in a house; not only that it may animate all its parts and render its organs fit and useful for their actions, but also that it may hold the first place in ruling man's life, not alone with respect to the duties of his earthly life, but at the same time to arouse him to honor God.[4]

In this respect, the soul functions similarly to the heart, with which it is often equated in Scripture. The heart lies at the core of our being and gives rise to "the issues of life."[5] The heart, or the soul, is the impulse and guiding force in our being. It "animates" every aspect of our life and will "hold first place" in everything we do, with respect to both "the duties of this earthly life" and our relationship with God. From the image of God, located in the soul, springs the impulse to create culture, to work with material reality in meaningful ways in order to bring good things into being, just as God Himself does. Those who are involved in the creation of popular culture are responding to an impulse within their souls which they may only vaguely understand, if at all, but which drives them to write music, play instruments, produce dramas, create films, and engage in the many other forms and expressions of popular culture as part of a personal quest for meaning in life. That impulse is the Spirit of God, working in and upon the soul, to incite people to seek the Lord and serve Him with all their heart, mind, and strength.[6]

At bottom, therefore, popular culture has its origins in the souls of men and women. For this reason, all popular culture has something inescapably religious about it. As Edmund Clowney notes, and as we have previously observed:

> Every culture has at its core a view of life and the world that is fundamentally religious, and that is expressed in social order as well as sacred practices. Yet no culture joins all its customs and social wisdom in one harmonious whole. Further, it is precisely at the heart of a culture that rebellion from God will be most evident.[7]

In part—perhaps large part—popular culture represents an attempt on the part of those who create and engage in it to bring some satisfaction to the longing of their soul, to find fulfillment and meaning, or to establish some kind of identity. For it is in the very nature of the soul to seek such things. God has made us for Himself, as Augustine reminds us, and our souls will be restless, striving, ever searching and seeking to find meaningful expression and fulfillment, until they find their rest in God.

At the same time, every individual's soul is uniquely his or hers. While it partakes of the image of God, it seeks expression through each individual in ways that are uniquely fitted to the person. This may help to explain why there is such great diversity in popular culture, as well as why the forms of popular culture mix and interact with one another so readily. The image of God in the human soul compels us to express our uniqueness in a search for full and meaningful life, in part through cultural activity. This is, in the end, a search for a relationship with God. As God the Creator made good things to bring blessing and wholeness to His creatures, so we, His image-bearers, following the urgings of our souls, create culture in all its forms to bless ourselves and others and to please God, however we may conceive of Him (even if our god is nothing more than mere self-gratification).

Popular culture springs from religious roots, from the image of God in people. Knowing this should raise questions in our minds about the religious quest and convictions of those who produce popular culture. And that should make us want to understand them and their concerns, and tell them about the rest that our souls have found in Jesus Christ.

The Gifts of God

As Calvin observed in the quote leading off this chapter, God has invested "notable endowments" in people, even in those who do not acknowledge or worship Him. The psalmist is crystal clear about this. God has distributed marvelous gifts among the men and women of the world, enabling them thereby to act upon the impulses of the

Spirit in their souls and to carry out their search for meaning and fullness in cultural activity. As Paul reminds us, echoing the psalmist, God's intention in this is that people might seek after Him and that He might dwell with them—that is, that they might know Him and live in a vital, abundant relationship of peace and love with Him. As men and women, driven by the impulses in their souls to discover meaning and purpose through culture (among other things), create the artifacts, institutions, and conventions of culture, God's intention is that they should not be satisfied with these as ends in themselves. Instead, His desire is that they should ever try to look beyond the works of their own hands to the giver of every good and perfect gift, who has set them on this quest and endowed them with gifts for making and enjoying culture.[8]

For all too many men and women, however, the quest never gets that far. In Romans 1:18-21, Paul explains what typically happens when people, following the impulse of the Spirit in their souls, set off on their quest for ultimate meaning and purpose. God has made it so that they know He exists. The manifestations of His goodness, greatness, majesty, glory, and divinity in the creation round about are utterly convincing, so much so that Paul can confidently say that all people know God, at least at the level of simple recognition. Yet, instead of showing gratitude to God for His many gifts and seeking a fuller understanding and richer relationship with Him, people turn away from Him, congratulate themselves on their cleverness and ability, and turn the objects of their culture into idols, to which they ascribe ultimate worth. The works of their hands—

whether pot-bellied images set beside a hearth or fat portfolios or the latest cultural diversion—become the objects of their devotion, that to which they give their energy, time, and resources, and from which they derive their joy and satisfaction. Meanwhile, God continues to surround rebellious people with His loving-kindness, in the form of gifts and other good things, even though they continue to deny Him, even to the extent of suppressing what knowledge of Him they do possess, and press on in their quest for full and meaningful life apart from Him.[9] God does not withdraw His good gifts; rather, He continues to supply them out of His great love for people, although He intends to hold all people accountable for how they have used those gifts—whether to honor and glorify themselves or Him.

Thus, again, the followers of Christ have much in common with those who create popular culture, apart from any sense of accountability to God. We are together the beneficiaries of His grace, for He causes His rain to fall and His sun to shine on the just and the unjust alike.[10] The many strange, wondrous, creative, thrilling, and remarkable abilities and products on display in the popular culture have their source, at least in part, in the good gifts of God. He has richly endowed men and women from all walks of life with capabilities that only human beings possess. His intention in this is that people might recognize His grace in the many gifts with which they are endowed and might seek to know, love, and serve Him with all their heart, mind, and strength.[11] That so many have failed to do so is no fault of God's; rather, their own sin and self-centeredness lead them to seek happiness in life apart from their Creator. At the same time, the presence of God's gifts in those who create the forms of popular culture should lead us to reflect on His goodness and look for ways of giving thanks and praise to Him.

Environment and Training

The artifacts, institutions, and conventions of popular culture arise within particular contexts as men and women, shaped in part by their environment and training, apply their knowledge and outlook to the creation of cultural forms that are meaningful to them. All culture is learned. "People are not born with a culture, a new way of life, but are nurtured into one."[12] This point will become particularly important later on in our discussion. For now, let us simply note that popular culture does not spring to life in a vacuum; rather, it shows the influence of many social and moral factors–home life, education, cultural heroes, contemporary issues and trends, and so forth. To a certain extent, popular culture is a reflection of the environment within which it emerges. At the same time, it serves to shape that environment and to influence the larger culture of which it is a part.

As we seek to understand popular culture, therefore, it will be important to determine what the significant influences on its forms and on those who produce them have been. What worldview most influences this writer, producer, or composer? Where was he or she trained, and what in particular about that training seems to be exerting the greatest influence? In this regard, every form of popular culture is an extension, development, or restatement of some earlier form, trend, or worldview. As such, the forms of contemporary popular culture can help us to identify ongoing trends and traditions and to think about where these might be headed or how we might benefit from them in the light of their earlier and most recent manifestations. The songs of Woody Guthrie, for example, with their celebrations of the dignity of life among the common people in America, sought to capture a vision of simplicity and individual greatness that the depression of the 1930s threatened to erase. Guthrie's work expressed in simple yet memorable tunes a long-standing tradition of the "common man" that had its roots in the earliest days of America—Jefferson's citizen farmers, the rude militiamen of New England who stood against the oppressive and sophisticated armies of England, Tocqueville's ethical and industrious farmers and merchants—and was further developed in the writings of such people as Walt Whitman and the social activities of labor organizers like Mother Jones. Woody Guthrie had an enormous influence on Bob Dylan, whose music in the 1960s sought to rally the common man and woman to stand up against injustice and forge a new direction for American society.[13] Dylan's lyrics were considered radical, even a threat, by many in the older generation, but they were in many respects nothing more than an extension of a venerable popular tradition into a new and confusing social situation. And they had profound effects upon an entire generation.

Other creators of popular culture have been shaped and influenced by the writings of great philosophers (I have already mentioned the influence of Marxist thinking on the later John Lennon), religious leaders, or novelists and playwrights. Unless we understand something about these influences, we will be hard-pressed to make sense of much of popular culture. Our tendency will be more to dismiss it than to appreciate it, and such an approach will not serve us well in seeking to engage it and its creators for the sake of the kingdom of Christ.

The Corrupting Effects of Sin

It is indisputable that sin has had a shaping hand in much of contemporary popular culture. The laments, tirades, and warnings that we so often hear from more conservative elements in our society bear ample testimony to this. Sin is a condition of rebellion against God, of turning away in ingratitude from His grace and care and seeking to forge a way in life apart from His guiding influence. Sin seeks to exalt the self, to promote ideas of freedom, self-expression, and authenticity that too quickly degenerate into licentiousness and moral upheaval as they come to expression in cultural forms. The influence of sin makes itself felt in the creation of popular culture along three avenues.

The world. The first avenue is that of the world—what Yeats called the *spiritus mundi,* the spirit of the age. The contemporary world spirit is largely naturalistic, individualistic, self-indulgent, and disdainful of restraints, except in the most pragmatic sense. Recent developments in the *spiritus mundi* have reintroduced significant elements of pagan religion as well. This tends to foster a popular culture that wants to smash the icons of tradition, overturn accepted values, justify all manner of self-indulgence, and foment a kind of moral and cultural anarchy. Contemporary popular culture exalts the pragmatic individual who forges his or her own way in life, apart from any restraints of tradition or social expectation. It minimizes the role of traditional values and institutions, relegating them to the status of nagging mother, while it seeks to make room for innovation and experimentation in individual moral conduct. Much of contemporary popular culture exalts sensuality at the expense of reason, self-expression over moral reflection, and immediate gratification over duty, devotion, or discipline. In so doing, popular culture both reflects the *spiritus mundi* and reinforces and shapes it further. As young people listen to contemporary popular music, watch sitcoms and movies, and read the magazines that comment on these, their sense of what life is all about is shaped in the direction of the spirit of the age, and they are encouraged to strike out on their own course of individual self-expression and self-indulgence. Thus, popular culture serves to mold not only how people feel and think, but how they feel and think about feeling and thinking, as Ken Myers puts it.[14] Popular culture reflects a particular worldview to those who partake of it, and then enlists them in the further realization and extension of that worldview, one shaped more by the law of sin than the law of God.

The flesh. Both giving rise to and feeding on the spirit of the age is the influence of the flesh, or what Scripture refers to as simple animal lust.[15] The lust of the flesh wages war against the spiritual interests of God, inducing people to follow base self-interest and sensual gratification over any sense of obligation to divine truth.[16] This passionate conviction arises from within the person, where the law of sin blocks out and distorts God's self-revelation in the creation and urges people on in the pursuit of experiences and ends that are not honoring to Him.[17] When the prophets and bards of popular culture declare that they "can't get no satisfaction," they are merely bearing testimony to the ultimate emptiness of fleshly lust. But they are also witnessing to its staying power. Apart from the redeeming work of Christ and the indwelling Spirit of God, men and women have no strength to resist the lust of the flesh, except whatever leftover influence of tradition or upbringing may be constraining them. And because this is continuously under attack by the spirit of the age, it is gradually eroded, leaving even the most upright and moral individuals susceptible to the pull of mere self-indulgence and self-gratification. The lust of the flesh finds encouragement in the contemporary *spiritus mundi* and thus sees little to restrain its every fantasy. Many of the forms of contemporary popular culture both express and encourage such an approach to life, giving free reign to the corrupting effects of sin.

The devil. We must acknowledge the role of Satan in the creation of certain forms of popular culture. There can be little doubt, it seems to me, that where gratuitous violence is exalted, social upheaval is advocated, and radical self-indulgence is made the final standard for life, a spirit is at work which is diametrically opposed to the Spirit of God. At the same time, I think we in the Christian community are sometimes too quick to ascribe Satanic influence to everything we find disagreeable, disgusting, or disquieting in contemporary popular culture.[18] In a sinful age such as ours—indeed, in any age, but especially, it seems, our own—sinful men and women are capable of producing offensive, even dangerous, cultural forms, quite apart from any influence of the Evil One. His presence among us, however, as he stalks about like a roaring lion, seeking whom he may devour, does not help the situation.

We must not be naïve about popular culture, thinking that it is merely harmless or a passing fad. Much of it has its roots in worldviews that want nothing more than to throw off the rule of God, be done with His law, and leave each man and woman free to find the life that is most satisfying to him or her. Such thinking has begun to find its way into even the most staid and traditionally reliable bastions of American culture, such as the Supreme Court. The infamous "mystery passage" of the 1992 decision, *Planned Parenthood v. Casey,* is just one example of the way radical autonomy, celebrated in the popular culture, is sapping the strength of the larger culture on which we all depend.[19] The influence of the world, the flesh, and the devil is very strong in contemporary popular culture, and, as we begin to engage it, we run the risk of succumbing to these powerful forces unless our eyes are open to their presence and role.

The Power of God's Spirit

The final source of popular culture is the Spirit of God. He is at work in the world to bless and woo the lost and to enable the redeemed to serve God in all their personal and cultural endeavors.

That God's Spirit is at work among His own people to redeem popular culture is clear from the many and varied forms of popular culture that Christians are working in today. Music, film, popular literature, and television show evidence of a strong and growing Christian presence. However we may regard that witness to date, we cannot deny its reality. The rapid growth of Christian contemporary music, video and film, television and radio programming, and literature for young people and adults can only be explained, at least in part, as having the blessing of God. That there is much work yet to be done in this area is undeniable. Many of the forms of contemporary Christian popular culture are little more than sophisticated evangelistic tracts; others are so syrupy and predictable as to be unconvincing; still others suffer from a lack of quality or a shortsighted Christian worldview. Contemporary Christian popular culture needs to break out of its narrow, pietistic mold and begin to address the larger issues of life in a fallen world, speaking a message to the redeemed and the unsaved alike about the tragedy and devastation of sin, the power of grace to make all things new, and the inevitable victory of Christ's kingdom. It must become more prophetic in its posture and more devoted to perfecting, rather than merely copying, the forms of contemporary

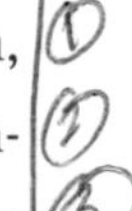

popular culture. But that the Spirit of God is at work here in many and varied ways seems to me undeniable.

At the same time, the Spirit of God is at work among those creators of popular culture who do not bow the knee to Jesus Christ. We have already commented on the widespread distribution of divinely given abilities among the creators of popular culture. God's Spirit works with those who possess those gifts to enable them to deploy them in remarkable, even brilliant, ways, even though they do not acknowledge the source of these gifts and may use them for ends other than those of the kingdom of God. How else can one explain the remarkable talents of a Carlos Santana, a George Lucas, or a Michael Jordan?

At the same time, God's Spirit works to restrain the sinful tendencies of men and women as they create the forms of popular culture, although, as their rebellion persists, He gives them up more and more to their sinful ways.[20] God's Spirit strives with sinful people, presumably so that they might acknowledge what they know to be true of Him from the revelation that surrounds them, and might seek to know Him more and more.[21] As people work with, in, and through the various forms of culture–including popular culture–God is testifying to them of Himself, urging them to give Him thanks and praise for His good gifts, and calling them to seek and to serve Him in all their ways. Whatever is good, pure, wholesome, and true in the popular culture–and there are many such manifestations–derives in part from the work of God's Spirit, exerting power for good, according to God's original intentions, against the corrupting influences of sin.

Thus, as we begin to engage popular culture for the purposes of Christ and His kingdom, we will want to be aware of the evidence of God's Spirit at work in and on the producers of that culture. We will remark on the Spirit's gifts, extol His virtues, and comment on the expressions of His good pleasure, while commending those who have created such forms in spite of themselves.

Mixed Motives, Mixed Results

As should be clear by now, the roots of popular culture extend widely. Its forms and expressions derive from numerous sources, acknowledged and unacknowledged, and this helps to explain the diversity of expressions that satisfy the insatiable appetites of those who are involved in it. As we begin to engage the popular culture for the sake of our kingdom calling in Christ, we will want to learn as much as possible about the sources of individual expressions of popular culture and the people who participate in it. This will allow us to have greater understanding, empathy, compassion, and patience as we work with them, and it will help us to keep from being overwhelmed by the forms of popular culture as they bring their messages and influence to bear upon us. This will be no easy undertaking, by any means. Yet it is absolutely necessary if we are to fulfill our calling in Christ's kingdom of exercising dominion over the earth, taking everything captive for Him, and reconciling the world to God.

But merely understanding the sources of any particular form of popular culture is less than half the battle. On that foundation we need to move forward to the adoption of a kingdom approach to popular culture, beginning with a clearer understanding of the kinds of standards we must employ. With an introductory understanding of the sources of popular culture, we may turn now to consider the standards that we must develop in order to evaluate and benefit from it.

Study Questions

1. How much do you know about the creators of popular culture whom you admire? What sources seem to be influencing their work? In what ways can you glimpse the impulses of God's Spirit in their creations?
2. How might having a clearer understanding of such sources help you to evaluate more carefully the forms of popular culture that give you pleasure? How would you begin to gain a better understanding of those sources?
3. What influences have affected your own involvement in popular culture? What in your background, training, or experience leads you to enjoy some forms of popular culture more than others? Is it possible that any of these influences may be antithetical to your calling in the kingdom of Christ? Can you give an example?
4. How might understanding the sources of popular culture help you in talking with an unsaved friend about his or her involvement in popular culture?

5. Review the goals you set for this study at the end of chapter 1. Are you making any progress in attaining them? In what ways? How has your study of popular culture from a kingdom perspective encouraged you thus far?

Four

Judging Popular Culture

In one's very perception of beauty, it delights and elevates the senses, and the mind. As an end in itself, beauty tends also to point by analogy to the divine, the first and final source of all beauty, and of truth and goodness and integrity, too.

—Frank Burch Brown[1]

Judge not according to the appearance, but judge righteous judgment.

—John 7:24

Before we can hope to benefit from popular culture for the purposes of our callings in the kingdom of Christ, we must articulate and adopt some standards that are consistent with our biblical worldview and mission. Such standards will allow us to exercise critical judgment with respect to popular culture as we engage its various forms and relate to those who are immersed in it.[2] We must make decisions about the forms of popular culture with which we are confronted, and in which we choose to participate, pronouncing some of them worthwhile and useful to our kingdom calling, and others unworthy of our walk with the Lord and unfruitful for our mission. As Ken

Myers observes, the cultural forms that "deny, suppress, or distort" the divine order "ought to be recognized as inferior to those that acknowledge, honor, and enjoy it."[3] As the sons and daughters of God, citizens of His kingdom, we are appointed to judge the earth and everything in it, and this includes the forms of popular culture.[4]

Some readers may have difficulty with the idea of rendering judgments about popular culture, since we have been commanded to "judge not, that ye be not judged," and since we should "judge nothing before the time, until the Lord come."[5] Judgment, such readers will argue, belongs to the Lord; it is not ours to criticize or condemn.

However, there are three solid arguments against such a nonjudgmental approach to popular culture.

We judge works of culture, not souls. When we judge the forms of popular culture that come our way, we are not pronouncing on the eternal disposition of their creators or promulgators, or of those who participate in such forms. The purpose of judging popular culture is not to condemn to eternal damnation those who make or use it. It is not our intention to make pronouncements on the eternal destination of their souls, but only on the works of their minds and hands, as well as our own. In order not to be "tossed to and fro, and carried about with every wind of doctrine,"[6] the church must cultivate discernment in all matters. We want to build our house of faith with solid rock and precious metals, not with wood, hay, and stubble, and this will require some exercise of sound judgment about the forms of popular culture and much else besides.[7]

Judgment is not optional. We cannot help but judge popular culture. There is just too much of it for us to indulge in all of it; in choosing some to enter into, we are inevitably exercising a form of judgment. For most of us, that judgment will be more on the order of a "gut feeling" or personal preference, apart from much informed biblical reasoning. We like what we like, take pleasure in what pleases us, and let the rest go, not always without some attitude or word of denunciation. In so doing, we are already exercising judgment on the forms of popular culture. This is an inescapable feature of cultural life. What I want to argue in this chapter is that we will exercise *better* judgment if the standards we use in making decisions about the forms of popular culture are more in keeping with the nature of our calling in the kingdom of God.

Jesus commands discernment. The Lord Jesus commands us to exercise *sound* judgment about many things that come our way each day. But He insists that such judgment be made on the basis of righteousness, that is, that which conforms to the character and purposes of God. We are to exercise "righteous judgment" with respect to the forms of popular culture, and not simply to dismiss them summarily or embrace them uncritically. But to do this we will need to have clearly and constantly in mind some criteria of righteousness—of the character of God—that relate specifically to our involvement in popular culture. The purpose of this chapter is to mark out some parameters for such standards that can better equip us to enter into popular culture without compromising our calling in Christ.

FIGURE 4.1.

THREE-LEGGED STOOL AND BRACES

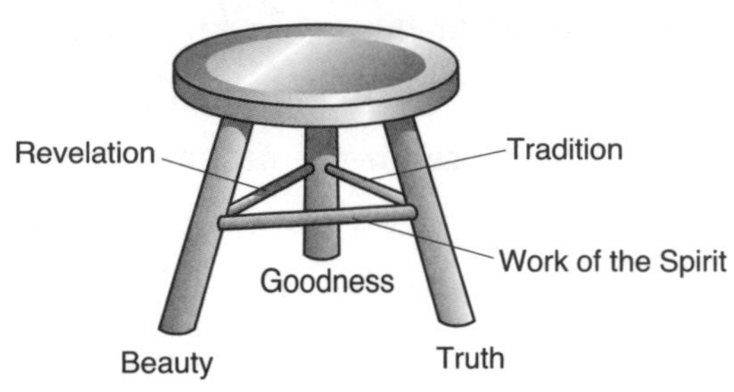

Three standards, or groups of standards, must be in place if we are to judge righteous judgment with respect to the forms of popular culture. They serve as the "legs" of our judgment seat. These are an understanding of beauty, a commitment to truth, and a devotion to goodness. All culture operates on the basis of such ideas, even if they are only highly individualized. But, as we have seen, mere individualism in such matters does not well serve the purposes of Christ and His kingdom. Therefore, these legs must be braced by three supports–God's revelation (in creation and Scripture), Christian tradition, and the ongoing work of the Holy Spirit. We sit to judge contemporary popular culture humbly, on a three-legged stool, as it were, the legs and braces of which must be strong and carefully linked in order for us to make sound judgments (see figure 4.1).

The three legs of beauty, goodness, and truth are supported by the three braces of revelation, tradition, and the work of the Spirit. These will provide a working foundation for judging our involvement in popular culture as citizens of the kingdom of God.

In addition, we cannot escape the question of taste, that is, of individual preference, when it comes to the question of how we shall engage popular culture. Each of us is unique as a creature made in the image of God. We see things differently, have somewhat different callings, find pleasure in different cultural forms and activities, encounter different expressions of culture, and will grow through our involvement in popular culture at different paces and in different ways. We cannot ignore the issue of taste, for, while taste is highly individual and subjective, it is not always valid. Further, taste can be cultivated and expanded. Each citizen of the kingdom of God, therefore, is responsible to cast a critical eye on, as well as to cultivate, his or her cultural taste according to the character and purposes of God's kingdom and his or her calling in that great undertaking.

In this chapter, we will explore each of these issues in an introductory manner, and then, in the next chapter, consider an approach to popular culture that allows us to employ these standards in the task of exercising righteous judgment with respect to contemporary popular culture.

Three Legs

Beauty, goodness, and truth are in the eye of the beholder, so we are told. This old cliché was perhaps never more true than in our postmodern society, where, as far as popular culture (among many other things) is concerned, every person is invited to embrace what seems right to him or her. What Arthur C. Danto has written about the arts in general is manifestly true with respect to popular culture: "So the contemporary is, from one perspective, a period of information disorder, a condition of perfect aesthetic entropy. But it is equally a period of quite perfect freedom. Today there is no longer any pale of history. Everything is permitted."[8] In the postmodern world, each individual is encouraged to be judge and jury over the forms of popular culture according to his or her own preferences and tastes, within the context of his or her chosen group or groups. There are no longer any absolute standards for art to which all artists must conform. Art is in the eye of its maker or its beholder. It should not surprise us, therefore, that Danto has announced "the end of art," for, if anything and everything is art, then nothing is art—at least, not as we have always known it. In postmodern thinking, the beholder rules supreme, and the popular culture, in recognition of this situation, proliferates forms and varieties of cultural artifacts to satisfy every whim and desire.

But the Christian must not be content with a merely individualistic perspective. Instead, he or she must ask who the *ultimate* beholder is. Christians are discouraged from looking only to themselves for answers to questions of beauty, goodness, and truth. We are told not to lean on our own understanding; that there is a way that seems right to us, but which ends up disastrously; and that our own hearts are deceitful and desperately wicked.[9] At the same time, Christians are called to be well aware of developments in the world around them, and to take those into consideration as they work in the kingdom of Christ.[10] These developments and perspectives are to be "tested" to see how much they reflect the truth of the world as God has created and entered into it for His saving purposes.[11] We must, then, be prepared to judge the forms of culture that confront us each day, and we must do so in the light of our sense of who we are and what we have been called to as citizens of the kingdom of God.

The Christian, therefore, recognizes that God Himself is the ultimate beholder of all culture, and must be allowed to serve as the final judge of cultural matters.[12] He alone can guide us in understanding the true nature of beauty, goodness, and truth. All that we do in the kingdom of God is to be done "in the name of the Lord," "to the glory of God," and to give pleasure and delight to Him as the primary audience.[13] In the final analysis, the Christian must seek to please God above all others in his or her involvement with popular culture.

Such a statement implies that God treasures certain standards of beauty, goodness, and truth, and that it is possible for the Christian to know and understand those standards and to apply them as he or she participates in the forms of popular culture that confront us each day.

These three issues–beauty, goodness, and truth–are intimately and inextricably linked in any cultural artifact. Yet, while it is difficult to separate them in judging any of the forms of popular culture, we may nonetheless recognize the distinctive character or concern of each, so that we may begin to consider the various forms that we encounter from the perspective of each of them. Beauty relates to matters of *aesthetics*, raising such questions as, Of what aesthetic quality or character is this cultural form? Is it truly beautiful? Moderately beautiful? Manifestly ugly? How effective and how skillful is the use of the particular genre or form in any specific example of popular culture? Goodness may be regarded as relating to the question of *ends:* For what purpose was this cultural form produced, and does it achieve its desired end? How, and to what extent? In what ways is that end consistent or at odds with the kingdom purposes of God? Truth relates to the question of *morality* and the *message* or *meaning* of any cultural form. Does this form express truth? Does it do violence to truth? In what ways? How are we to receive and interpret the meaning or message of this form? How must we respond to it?

The Christian must have a growing understanding of how such questions may be answered in the context of the kingdom of God, as well as the skills of analysis and evaluation to determine the degree of beauty, goodness, and truth expressed through any particular form of pop culture. The question remains, however, as to how such standards are to be arrived at, and here we must get ahead of ourselves just a bit.

Fundamental to the Christian view of life is the idea that God has been pleased to reveal Himself and His good pleasure to human beings by way of both natural and special revelation—that is, both in the world He has made and in the Word He has spoken.[14] Most importantly, God's law and the writings and teachings of prophets, apostles, and the Lord Jesus Himself portray standards of truth and goodness that leave little room for guessing about what pleases God.

At the same time, the creation around us is constantly telling of the glory of God, of what pleases Him. It speaks to us in magnificent terms about such matters as beauty, propriety, tragedy, injustice, and a host of other subjects. Therefore, in addition to careful study of God's Word, more attention to the forms and processes of the natural world might also yield fruitful substance for the standards we require in judging popular culture. This study of the creation—looking for examples and norms of beauty, goodness, and truth—is the proper calling of kingdom citizens, yet it may be carried out effectively only in the light of special revelation.[15] Notions not only of goodness and truth, but of beauty as well, might be coaxed out of our study of the creation in the light of God's Word.

This twofold revelation has been received, interpreted, and applied throughout the history of God's covenant people, who have left exceedingly helpful summaries, explanations, and examples of how to think about (among many other things) such ideas as beauty, goodness, and truth. Thus, we may believe that a great many questions of right and wrong, good and evil, acceptable and unacceptable, can be resolved merely by more attentive study of the Word of God in the light of the conclusions of our forebears in the faith. Resolving these questions beforehand can aid us immensely as we begin to engage the forms of popular culture. Here we are anticipating ourselves, as we shall have more to say about these "braces" shortly. For now, however, our focus on the question of beauty, goodness, and truth, as they are pleasing to God, will not allow us to avoid having to deal with what He has revealed to us about such matters, together with how our forebears have regarded this revelation.

Thus, we should expect both Scripture and God's revelation in the creation to speak to us concerning what pleases Him. The Christian would do well to be a devout student of both these "books" if he or she is to penetrate the mind of God with respect to the question of standards for judging popular culture.[16]

In particular, where God has brought into focus *both* revelational media—the created world and the revealed Word—in expressing His mind regarding beauty, goodness, and truth, the Christian may hope to discern, if only in broad outline, principles for judging popular culture. We may thereby determine which aspects of it are pleasing to God and, thus, consistent with His plan for all His creatures and beneficial to their mission in the kingdom of God. And, while many places in Scripture reveal such a confluence of revelational media, this may be seen especially to occur in such passages as Genesis 1 and 2, Isaiah 60, and Revelation 21.

In Genesis 1, God over and over comments on the work of His hands—which we might, without too much strain on our imaginations, be able to envision—as being "good" or pleasing in His sight, because it pleased Him to look upon it, and it fulfilled the purposes He intended in making it. In chapter 2, He further describes His ideal environment for His most precious creatures, going even so far as to mention the beauty of certain aspects of it and to declare certain truths by which that beauty and goodness were to be sustained.

In Isaiah 60 and Revelation 21, God projects a vision in creational terms of the ideals of beauty, goodness, and truth that He will bring into being in the new heavens and new earth. Without seeking to establish concise definitions of these three notions, we may briefly summarize what these passages suggest to us concerning the ideas of beauty, goodness, and truth that satisfy the requirements of the divine beholder in judging culture in any of its many forms.

What do we find in these passages? We encounter

- images of harmony amid diversity;
- order superintending a plurality of forms;
- hierarchies of value (gold and precious gems, peace as opposed to war, holiness instead of sin, individual responsibility in the light of God's revealed will);
- the use of recognizable subjects and forms, yet the freedom to employ them in hyperbolic or imaginal manner for effect (a child playing by a snake's hole, an exaggerated description of a city);
- hints of as yet undisclosed beauty and goodness (trees that bear fruit, precious gems in the ground);
- contrasts and combinations of light and color;
- progress and development;
- counsel concerning proper affections and aspirations (do not eat this, do that);
- the contextualizing of what is ugly and evil by comparison with what is pleasing to God and beneficial for His creatures (the necessity of "guarding" the garden against some unknown intruder, the banishing of tears and death);

- an overall environment that both satisfies the divine will and appeals to an inherent sense of beauty in men and women (trees "beautiful to look at").

In the light of these few passages, we might be able to conclude, at least preliminarily, that beauty consists in diversity and harmony of forms, colors, textures, and materials, within an overall scheme in which everything has its place, nothing is superfluous, everything exists in proper proportion and relation to everything else, and everything conforms to the divine intentions for the creation. Goodness appears to be that which skillfully and efficiently expresses the character and satisfies the pleasure of God and advances His purposes, which are, primarily, to make Himself known and to exalt His glory. Truth resides in God's declared will for the use of all that He has made and, in particular, the place of people in His economy–that they should live within the parameters of His revealed will, being content and fulfilled in knowing His blessings and serving Him.

Such descriptive phrases do not exhaust the definitions of beauty, goodness, and truth that we must employ in judging the culture around us. However, they can be seen to point in the direction of fuller definitions and, at the very least, can stand as touchstones to which Christians, eager above all else to please God in their use of culture, may resort in judging and participating in the popular culture around them.

Does this mean that there is no place for that which is ugly in our involvement with popular culture? Or for that which rebels against God and His truth? Or those forms which thrive on disorder, chaos, and confusion? Not necessarily. It simply means that, with a clearer sense of what we mean by beauty, goodness, and truth, we will have standards available to make such observations for what they are, to locate the forms representing them according to our own cultural outlook, and to decide intelligently how we may best employ such cultural forms (if at all).

We may note that great Christian artists of the past have been well aware of the need for standards of beauty, goodness, and truth, and have sought—in their own generations and cultural activity—to work faithfully within them. Even more, they have found such standards to derive from careful consideration of both Scripture and the created world. This can be seen by a brief consideration of two such artists, the sixteenth-century painter Albrecht Dürer and the nineteenth-century poet Gerard Manley Hopkins.

Dürer, for example, warned aspiring artists against following their own tastes alone in expressing beauty, goodness, and truth, and encouraged them to study both the Scriptures and the created world. He concluded from his own (prodigious) work in these areas that such things as harmony, a proper blending of colors, right proportion and true measurement, and faithful representation of nature as God created it are the surest ways to attain beauty, goodness, and truth in the arts.[17] He wrote:

> Much learning is not evil to a man, though some be stiffly set against it, saying that art puffeth up. Were that so, then were none prouder than God who hath performed all arts. But that cannot be, for God is perfect in

> goodness. The more, therefore, a man learneth so much the better doth he become, and so much the more love doth he win for the arts and for things exalted.[18]

Dürer counseled humility and continual diligence in the development of one's own abilities, insisting that the attainment of true beauty in the arts was an extremely difficult task. He was a diligent student of God's Word all his life and allowed his understanding of Scripture to have a formative role in his own work as artist, teacher, and proponent of church reform. And he counseled those who would become involved in the arts to take seriously the study of what the world around us can reveal about the true nature of beauty, goodness, and truth.

Hopkins, in his "On the Origin of Beauty: A Platonic Dialogue," came to very similar conclusions. He judged that symmetry, diversity, orderliness, faithful use of color, careful representation of the natural world, and a prudent use of images were the most reliable ways of achieving beauty in art. Here is a portion of the dialogue between two gentlemen who are leisurely discussing the nature of beauty as they observe chestnut and oak leaves:

> "Then the beauty of the oak and the chestnut-fan and the sky is a mixture of likeness and difference or agreement and disagreement or consistency and variety or symmetry and change."
>
> "It seems so, yes."
>
> "And if we did not feel the likeness we should not think them so beautiful, or if we did not feel the difference we should not think them so beautiful. The

> beauty we find is from the comparison we make of the things with themselves, seeing their likeness and difference, is it not?"[19]

Like Dürer, Hopkins (a Jesuit priest) was a devout student of Scripture and scrupulous in his exercise of spiritual disciplines. He was also a careful observer of the world around him. Many of his poetic themes express his biblical understanding of the world. He believed that beauty, goodness, and truth disclosed themselves to those with faith and an eye for careful observation. Most of us, however, are too immersed in the business of using the creation for our own selfish ends to take the time to consider what God might be saying to us through it. His poem "God's Grandeur" captures these sentiments admirably.

> The world is charged with the grandeur of God.
> It will flame out, like shining from shook foil;
> It gathers to a greatness, like the ooze of oil
> Crushed. Why do men then now not reck his rod?
> Generations have trod, have trod, have trod;
> And all is seared with trade; bleared, smeared with toil;
> And wears man's smudge and shares man's smell: the soil
> Is bare now, nor can foot feel, being shod.
>
> And for all this, nature is never spent;
> There lives the dearest freshness deep down things;

And though the last lights off the black West went
  Oh, morning, at the brown brink eastward,
    springs–
Because the Holy Ghost over the bent
  World broods with warm breast and ah! bright
    wings.

No one will deny that Dürer and Hopkins were and will long be recognized as masters of their chosen callings and contributors to a culture that is pleasing to God. They produced works of enduring beauty, goodness, and truth from which many subsequent generations of artists have benefited in working to perfect their craft. Both of these men were serious students of Scripture and careful observers of the world around them. They were also diligent workers at their craft, seeking from many sources and resources guidance, insight, and skill in the development of their technique. And their views on what constitutes beauty, goodness, and truth in art resonate quite well with what we observed in Genesis, Isaiah, and Revelation to be the preferences of the divine beholder with respect to these matters.

Thus, we must ask of any form of popular culture, To what extent does it represent or conform to those standards of beauty, goodness, and truth that God Himself might find pleasurable? Is there something about this or that form that reveals or points to something in the character of God, or in the world as He made it, or as it is truly constituted now, this side of the Fall? Does it evidence variegation and harmony within a general format of order and purpose? To what specific purpose is the work devoted? How well does it achieve that purpose? What is its ultimate truth-claim? Is evil identified as such or made to be something other than what God's Word says it is? Is righteousness extolled or cast aside? Does the culture maker in question make skilled and creative use of the techniques and technologies of his or her chosen form? How does that use compare with other similar expressions of popular culture? How might this form serve our purposes and callings in the kingdom of God?

Our involvement in popular culture, as citizens of the kingdom of God and followers of Jesus Christ, must be decided according to norms of beauty, goodness, and truth that we feel confident would be pleasing to God. Every cultural form recommends some understanding of what is beautiful, good, and true. The intense appeal of popular culture to mere self-gratification can obscure our thinking and lead us to use forms of pop culture for purely selfish reasons. But such can never be pleasing to God. Only what is pleasing to God will suffice for every aspect of our lives. Thus, we must be diligent to ask, concerning any form of pop culture, What is its sense of beauty? How does it fulfill the purposes of goodness? What does it want me to receive as truth? And we must hold the popular culture accountable for its claims and products according to standards of beauty, goodness, and truth that will delight the divine eye as well as our own. These three legs—beauty, goodness, and truth—must ever come into play as we engage the popular culture around us.

But they must never come into play apart from the

braces of revelation, tradition, and the ongoing work of God's Spirit.

Three Braces

As there are three legs on our modest cultural judgment seat, so there are three braces that, firmly connected to one another and to each of the legs, must be allowed to inform and guide our thinking about the standards of righteous judgment we will use in engaging the forms of popular culture.

We have already mentioned two of those braces—God's revelation and the interpretive tradition in which that revelation has been received and applied. Here is not the place to argue for the foundational role of revelation—created revelation interpreted in the light of special, biblical revelation—or the secondary, but essential role of Christian tradition in understanding and making use of that revelation. Suffice it to say that, unless our judgments in any area of life are grounded in God's revelation and are consistent with the tradition of Christian thought and practice, we are in danger of making our judgments on shaky and uncertain ground.[20] Kingdom citizens must order their lives according to kingdom decrees, illustrated by the King's self-revelation in the world, and guided by kingdom forebears whose labors have been blessed of God in their own day and time. These two braces—revelation and Christian tradition—will be of enormous help in allowing us to think about matters of beauty, goodness, and truth as they relate to the question of our involvement in popular culture, as we have seen. Without them, we are left to our own best judgments, which are likely to be ultimately self-serving and tossed about by every wind and whim of contemporary doctrine and belief. Without solid building blocks cut from the Rock of revelation and mortared with the cement of tradition, we shall have only whatever wood, hay, and stubble may be at our immediate disposal for building our kingdom enterprise for the Lord.

Here, obviously, there is much work to be done. Contemporary Christians are not accustomed to reading the Scriptures with an eye to matters of culture. Nor are they familiar with the many resources of the Christian heritage that can be of use to us in controlling the kudzu of popular culture. It is the responsibility of pastors and teachers to lead the people of God in developing a more critical understanding of such issues, and in deploying standards of judgment that are consistent with what Scripture and the Christian tradition recommend.

The third brace that must be firmly in place is some awareness of the ongoing work of the Holy Spirit, both in the church and in the world. God's Spirit is ever at work illuminating His Word in new ways in the changing circumstances of history and culture. This means that the Christian tradition is an ongoing project and will exhibit continuous development. At the same time, God's Spirit is continuing to give cultural gifts to believers and nonbelievers alike. He is at work doing new things in the cultural realm, and we must learn to be alert to areas and ways in which He may be working. In each generation, thinkers, artists, and other creators—prompted, at least in part, by the Spirit of God—are discovering new ways of making use of cultural forms to express their understanding of beauty, goodness, and truth.

Those medieval monks who invented musical notation and the eight-note scale must certainly have been following the Holy Spirit as He guided them to improve through innovation the use of existing cultural forms for the purposes of God's kingdom. Christian poets such as Petrarch, Spenser, and Milton, who invented and perfected the sonnet, or Dante, who mastered the *terza rima* form, have set standards for all generations of English poets, Christian and non-Christian alike. Those Catholic and Protestant painters who perfected the use of *chiaroscuro* in the seventeenth century established new ways of using light that many subsequent painters have sought to emulate.[21]

In these and many other cases, spiritually sensitive people, operating on the basis of Scripture and tradition, responded to a new moving of the Spirit in their day and their lives, and blazed new trails of cultural development for generations to come. A contemporary analogy may be the contemporary Christian music movement, which, while it leaves much to be desired, is nonetheless experimenting and pointing the way to taking the forms of rock music captive for the kingdom purposes of God. Surely God's Spirit is at work among these musicians to enable His people to sing a new song to Him.

Here we want to be sure that we are able to respond to the Lord's call to sing that "new song," one that, based on

Scripture and located within the Christian tradition, garners contemporary forms, or creates new ones, as vehicles through which the Spirit of God can impress divine notions of beauty, goodness, and truth on the people of every age. At the same time, we want to be able to identify indications of His working among the masters of popular culture in the communities of the unsaved, be they ever so defective, for all the purposes of cultural involvement that we will examine in our final chapter.

These three braces–revelation, tradition, and the ongoing work of the Spirit–are rich sources of understanding for developing kingdom ideas of beauty, goodness, and truth. The Christian who engages the popular culture apart from these is in danger of being drawn away from his or her kingdom calling into a life of dissipation, disappointment, and ultimate despair. Therefore, it behooves us, as we sit humbly to judge the forms of popular culture, to have these legs and braces firmly in place and vitally interconnected.

The Question of Taste

The huge diversity of popular culture makes the question of taste of critical importance. For no matter what one's taste–in music, film, television programming, or any other form of popular culture–one can be sure to find something to satisfy it. That can lead to the development of fairly narrow tastes, tastes reflective more of unexamined personal preference than carefully considered kingdom principles, or to fairly uncritical tastes, which can fertilize the kudzu of popular culture so that it threatens to overwhelm us.

According to Frank Burch Brown,

> Taste primarily has to do with aesthetic response and responsiveness. Yet it has three elements or facets: perceiving, enjoying, and judging–which I like to term "apperception," "appreciation," and "appraisal." Taste, in short, has to do with the various elements of aesthetic discernment and response.[22]

He continues:

> "Taste" brings to mind enjoyment, and possibly joy. Taste, then, unites delights with virtues. Good aesthetic taste values something intrinsically pleasing that, while valuable in its own right, is also good for human life.[23]

Brown argues persuasively for Christians to develop a level of taste that is consistent with their calling as citizens of the kingdom of God. This will take them beyond worldly standards of "good taste" and "bad taste"–conceived, perhaps, as the traditional distinction between "high culture" and "low culture"–to a level of taste that will allow them to enter with divine joy and kingdom benefit into a wide range of cultural experiences.

We might say three things about taste.

Taste is highly personal. This is both the good news and the bad news. That taste is highly personal is good in that each Christian can be encouraged to identify and develop his or her own tastes to the fullest. I don't have to like the same music as my son Casey, and he doesn't have to like mine. We are free to indulge our individual tastes and to be content in the consumption of our own cultural cuisine.

The bad news is that, besides possibly leading us into cultural activities and enjoyments that do not further our kingdom interests, our individualized tastes can tend to make us cultural snobs, denouncing or at least ignoring every form of popular culture that fails to suit our taste. The problem with this is that, in so doing, we can seem to condemn those for whom such forms are a source of meaning and pleasure. Unless Casey and I can learn to revel in our personal tastes and, at the same time, to respect, take an interest in, and try to understand one another's tastes, we shall have difficulty fulfilling the commandment to love our neighbor as ourselves. Moreover, unless we can manage to get beyond our own tastes to develop new ones—or, at least, to appreciate why others might—we shall have difficulty gaining an entrée for our kingdom mission among those whose tastes range far afield from the eternal purposes that occupy us.

Taste needs responsible direction. Each of us is responsible for our tastes and for what they lead us to indulge in, or what they lead us to become, before the Lord. Therefore, we must labor to ensure that our tastes are grounded in notions of beauty, goodness, and truth that have been carefully reached as part of our calling in God's kingdom, and are being properly exercised in our involvement with popular culture.

Thus, while we are free to indulge our personal tastes—within the parameters set by righteous judgment—we must be willing to refine and expand them, if only to make space in our cultural activities for engagement, conversation, and relationships with others whose tastes differ markedly from our own.

Taste can be developed. Brown writes, "At its highest, taste—as seen especially in the sense of beauty and in the sense of sublimity—enters into the sense of God and the sense of good."[24] Our desire must be so to cultivate our tastes that, increasingly, we see the vast, diverse world of culture as God does, and are able to perceive, appreciate, appraise, and enjoy a wide range of the forms of pop culture, without being overwhelmed by any of them, and to enjoy them, ultimately, for how they enhance our knowledge of God. Brown's book as a whole is a veritable handbook for developing distinctively Christian cultural tastes. For our purposes, and in our context, I wish to suggest that we can expect our taste in the area of popular culture to improve to the extent that

(1) we develop our kingdom understanding of the nature of beauty, goodness, and truth;
(2) we increase our familiarity with God's revelation, the Christian cultural tradition, and the work of the Holy Spirit among contemporary makers of culture; and

(3) we engage from our kingdom framework an increasingly wide range of the forms of pop culture, as well as the people for whom those forms have meaning and significance.

While it will be immediately apparent that these activities are intertwined and interrelated, I want to offer a few brief suggestions as to how one might proceed in each area.

First, with respect to the "legs" of our humble judgment stool: discussions of the nature and meaning of beauty, goodness, and truth abound in the pages of cultural history. Among those writing from a Christian perspective, besides Dürer and Hopkins, such names as Matthew Arnold, T. S. Eliot, Hans Rookmaaker, C. S. Lewis, Leland Ryken, Francis Schaeffer, and Nicholas Wolterstorff come to mind as sources that one might consult for additional insight into these matters. Their works suggest ways of thinking about such issues that can help to sharpen our own thinking.

Second, we can study the Scriptures more carefully for insights into these areas. By looking at the Word of God with a view to discerning its teaching regarding beauty, goodness, and truth, as these relate to cultural expressiveness, we will be surprised to find how much the Bible actually does have to say—not just in such obvious places as the Song of Songs, the descriptions of the tabernacle and the temple, and certain of the psalms, but in many other places as well. The book of Lamentations, for example, is a beautiful, albeit tragic, literary tableau of such complete devastation that we might, by inferring its opposite, come to a better understanding of how God intends us to use culture for His good ends and according to His truth, rather than for mere self-indulgence.

We can also examine our current tastes in popular culture according to the standards of beauty, goodness, and truth that we are beginning to acquire, in order to test those tastes to see whether or how they might serve the purposes of our kingdom calling in Christ. Such an exercise in "testing the spirits" can develop into an ongoing discipline that can serve us well throughout our lives.

Finally, it behooves us to stay abreast of developments in the popular culture, which we can do by any number of means. Refusing to live within a "cultural cocoon," engaging in dialogue with other believers, reading critical assessments of popular culture, getting to know new people outside the church, and looking more critically at our own preferences in this realm, are just a few of the many activities in which we might profitably engage. We shall have more to say about these matters in the next chapter.

As we begin to develop standards of beauty, goodness, and truth that are consistent with the teaching of Scripture, the tradition of the church, and the moving of God's Spirit in the world of popular culture today, we will become more aware of our own tastes and better able to nurture them in a manner that is more consistent with the tastes of the divine beholder. This will put us in good stead to begin approaching the popular culture of our day according to our callings as citizens of the kingdom of God.

We may not simply assume that the tastes and preferences that we currently enjoy in the popular culture are either the best ones or the only ones from which we might benefit. Without carefully developed standards and a critical awareness of our own tastes, we shall have difficulty fulfilling the Lord's requirement that we judge righteously when we are involved in popular culture. A disability in this crucial area will be a continuing liability in our efforts to carry out our calling to see the kingdom of God come on earth as it is in heaven.

Study Questions

1. What standards currently guide your involvement with popular culture? How have you come to settle on those standards? Do you think those standards are adequate to allow you to realize your full potential as a servant of Christ's kingdom? Why or why not?
2. Think of a form of popular culture that gives you particular pleasure–a song, film, sport, or other form. What about that form would you describe as beautiful? Good? True? Listen to your answers: do they sound like the kind of answers that would give pleasure to God? Why or why not?
3. Prepare a catalog of your tastes in popular culture. Make a list of several forms of popular culture that give you pleasure. Make another list of those that you pay little or no attention to. Are your tastes for the things on these lists consciously determined using the kinds of standards talked about in this chapter?
4. Look at the list you made of the forms of popular culture in which you do not participate. Do you know

anyone who does? If that person is a Christian, how might some appreciation of those forms help you to fulfill your kingdom calling to love one another and stimulate one another to love and good works? If that person is not a Christian, how might some understanding or appreciation of those forms help you to be more effective in ministering to him or her?

5. Think of some ways in which you might begin to prepare yourself to be more effective at exercising righteous judgment. Where would you begin? What might your plan include? Is there someone you could work with in this effort? What would you hope to be the result of your effort?

Five

Approaching Popular Culture

The end that we are to seek is the redemption of our world—the world that is truly ours and of which we are ourselves a part. . . . Our role as Christians, as the people of the cross within that world, is precisely what Jesus said it was: to be salt, yeast, and light.
—Douglas John Hall[1]

Therefore if any man be in Christ, he is a new creature: old things are passed away; behold, all things are become new. And all things are of God, who hath reconciled us to himself by Jesus Christ, and hath given to us the ministry of reconciliation.
—2 Corinthians 5:17–18

At this point, some readers may have concluded that learning to take a kingdom approach to popular culture is just too much work. It requires too much vigilance. There is just too much to learn about beauty, goodness, and truth, as well as the teaching of Scripture and Christian tradition about such things. And it would appear to be an exercise in futility to try to discern the leading of the Spirit amid all the flotsam and jetsam of popular culture.

To a certain extent, I must concede that this is not an entirely inaccurate observation. Most of us no doubt find ourselves fully immersed in various aspects of the popular culture without ever having thought much about such questions as taste and truth as they relate to our personal preferences—except, perhaps, when it comes to the more egregious and offensive examples of popular culture. We like what we like, we don't see any harm in it, and so we don't feel any need to gear up for a more thoughtful attempt to reconcile our use of popular culture with the demands of our kingdom calling. It would simply take more time than we are willing to give.

However, as Christians we are called to redeem the time allotted to us each day.[2] We must not approach our use of time, and the activities that fill it, like the fool, who says in his heart, "There is no God"—that is, as if God is not concerned with the matters occupying my time at any particular moment.[3] Christians are called to live wisely in this present age, to trust in the Lord with *all* our heart, to commit *all* our ways to Him, so that He might have His good and perfect will in our lives.[4] We may not continue in the same darkened, hardened mind-set of unbelief that characterized us before the light of Christ began to shine in our hearts; rather, we must seek a renewing of our minds and embrace the changes in lifestyle that that will require.[5]

Thus, to opt for the status quo in our use of popular culture would be to deny our callings as salt, light, and yeast in a world pervaded by sin and rebellion against God. Salt, light, and yeast all have this much in common: they enter into everything they confront and establish a transforming presence. So it must be with Christians, called to be citizens of the heavenly kingdom, in every aspect of our lives in this world. We enter the world each day as a small but powerful influence, and must seek to establish a pervading presence and work hard to effect the kinds of transformation that result in the kingdom of God coming more forcefully on earth as it is in heaven.

I do not apologize, therefore, for throwing down the gauntlet in this chapter and the preceding one. Being a Christian is the most demanding way of life that anyone can follow, and no one should embark upon it without first counting the cost of being a disciple of the Savior. Part of that cost is the ongoing work of transformation—personal, social, and cultural—so that we may be effective agents of grace, being used of God to reconcile the world to Him. And if we are to reconcile our use of popular culture to the Lord, we must shake off the status quo, gird up our minds for action, and get on with the hard work of taking every thought captive for Jesus Christ.[6]

With that in mind, therefore, I want to outline six aspects of an approach to popular culture that will better enable us to realize our kingdom purpose in this inescapable area of life in postmodern society. A kingdom approach to popular culture will be one that is prayerful, intelligent, purposeful, critical, dialogical, and redemptive.

Approaching Popular Culture Prayerfully

As in everything, prayer must be the foundation of our approach to participating in popular culture.[7] In prayer, we orient our lives to God our King, examine ourselves and our activities in the light of His truth, seek grace to help in our times of need, find the clarification and guidance that He desires for us, and draw on His strength to be renewed in our whole being.

For some, it may seem trite to pray about our involvement in popular culture. We may suppose that God is busy with so much else, and that there are so many more important concerns to fill our fleeting moments of prayer, that we can't see the necessity of bothering Him with, or wasting our precious prayer time in, so trivial a matter. However, such an attitude reveals either that we do not understand the power of popular culture to exert a negative formative influence on our lives, or that we do not take seriously the command to pray about everything. Given what we know about the kudzulike power of popular culture, and given what we believe about the efficacy of prayer, we ought not to despise bringing this aspect of our lives before the throne of grace with increasing regularity and fervor.

But how should we pray? Allow me to suggest some ways to converse with the Lord about your participation in popular culture.

Pray for your involvement. Pray daily about what you anticipate to be your involvement with popular culture. You will be exposed to much advertising, the purpose of which is to challenge your stewardship over the wealth God has entrusted to you. Enticing songs will waft across your mind, suggesting thoughts, attitudes, and commitments that will not all be agreeable to your kingdom calling. Perhaps you will listen to the radio or watch television. All these influences are like the snares and traps concerning which the psalmist so often appealed to God for help.[8] Are you prepared for the messages of self-interest, self-indulgence, and self-seeking that they may present? Is there a danger that any of these aspects of the popular culture might woo or divert you, even if ever so slightly, from the commitments and path of the kingdom of God?

Certainly there is. Ask God to keep your mind alert to the various forms of popular culture that you will confront each day. Pray that He would enable you to see the traps and snares of temptation, to be aware of any incipient tendencies in your heart to love the world, to resist the devil as he encourages you to indulge yourself in a mindless, thoughtless manner, and to have His mind about the forms of popular culture that you will be involved with each day. Ask Him for wisdom in ordering your time each day, so that you might control the kudzu of popular culture that you will inevitably confront, rather than being overwhelmed by it.[9]

Pray about what you can learn. Seek the Lord's wisdom in understanding what He is revealing about Himself, the times in which you live, and the people around you in the various forms of popular culture. Remember that the ability to produce popular culture comes, at least in part, from the gifts that God has lavishly distributed upon all people. In these good gifts, we may see something of His beauty, goodness, and truth, even though these things have been obscured by the particular interests of our postmodern popular culture. There is light from God to be discerned in the popular culture, but we will only be able to recognize what He may be saying to us in the light of His wisdom, revealed in His Word.[10] As we seek the Lord in prayer, asking for His wisdom to be able to approach popular culture as citizens of His kingdom, we may expect Him to make Himself and His truth more perfectly known to us.[11] The various forms of popular culture can actually enhance and enrich our knowledge of God, our understanding of our mission and our ability to carry it out, and our delight in living in God's kingdom, as we shall see in the next chapter. But that will happen only as we seek God's wisdom regarding the popular culture, calling on Him to give us clear heads and penetrating insight as we search His Word and labor to control the kudzu of popular culture all around us.

Pray for those who shape culture. Pray for those who produce and distribute popular culture. Surely they are numbered among the "all men" whom Paul indicated to be the proper scope of our prayers.[12] That may seem like a tall order, but if we focus on those producers and promoters of popular culture in whom we are most interested–the musicians we enjoy, the actors and actresses we appreciate, the athletes we follow, and so forth–the task becomes more manageable. Pray that God's Spirit would strive with them, that they might see the Lord in the things around them, and cultivate hearts of gratitude toward Him.[13] Pray that they would not take God's wonderful loving-kindness for granted, but would see in their talents and abilities precious gifts from Him who loves them and desires them to seek Him.[14] Ask the Lord to open doors of opportunity for these people to hear the good news of Jesus Christ, and to open the eyes of their hearts so that they might come to understand and believe the gospel.[15] You might even pray that God would bring them to such confusion, disappointment, and sorrow that they would be led to seek Him, out of desperation.[16] If they are Christians, pray that God would brighten their light, make their salt more savory, and strengthen the leavening effects of their presence in the world of popular culture.

A kingdom approach to popular culture—as to anything else in our calling to exercise dominion over the earth—must begin with prayer. I have suggested just a few ways that prayer can begin to orient us more properly toward the task of controlling the kudzu of popular culture. You will discover other and more personally meaningful and relevant ways of praying for the producers and promoters of popular culture as well.

Approaching Popular Culture Intelligently

We must make sure that our involvement in popular culture is with an active, inquisitive mind, one that seeks understanding and is not easily tossed about and carried about by every wind of doctrine wafting in from the popular culture.

The sorry state of the evangelical mind has been long and loudly lamented.[17] Harry Blamires suggests that a "Christian mind" must be duly oriented to spiritual concerns, alert to the possibilities of evil, seeking God's truth in all things, submissive to proper authority (e.g., those who might teach us how to think about cultural matters), concerned for the well-being of people, and eager to discover the presence of God and the wonder of His grace in all things. He maintains that the absence of an informed and active Christian mind in our secular society has been a primary reason why so many young people over the past two generations have been dragged away in the nets of sensuality and materialism. Christian young people have not been immune to this allure. Clearly, if this situation is to be improved, Christians shall have to give themselves more diligently to perfecting the use of their minds.

This will require us to work in two directions at the same time.

Become more thoughtful. We shall have to improve our ability to engage contemporary forms of popular culture intellectually. We must labor for what James Sire calls "the perfecting of the mind."[18] In biblical parlance, we must "gird up" our minds for action as we begin to consider how best to control the kudzu of popular culture.[19]

James Sire's book, while written primarily for aspiring intellectuals, offers many helpful suggestions for those who want to improve their ability to think clearly about engaging popular culture. Our goal must be the pursuit of a perfected mind, one that "stretches itself around facts and discerns their relationships."[20] Sire insists that we must renounce our intellectual complacency and cultivate a passion for truth. He recommends that we spend time in solitude and silence, waiting on the Lord to give us understanding of the objects of our study. He urges us to pay careful attention to that with which we are engaged, suspending judgment as we seek understanding. He says that we must nurture the ability to "think laterally," that is, to look for the connections between things, comparing and contrasting ideas and points of view. Finally, we must bathe the entire process of study and contemplation in prayer. Here there is no substitute for reading, perhaps beginning with some of the excellent books written by Christian observers of popular culture cited in this volume, but considering the works of nonbelievers as well.

The only alternatives to taking a thoughtful approach to the forms of contemporary popular culture are either to follow the latest trend or to fall back on our established preferences. Neither of these will enable us to develop the intellectual strength that is essential to taking every thought captive in order to make it obedient to Jesus Christ.

Think more Christianly. At the same time, we need to learn how to "think Christianly" about the forms of popular culture with which we are daily engaged. We must not only develop the ability to understand popular culture, but also improve our ability to analyze it from a kingdom perspective on life. Jonathan Edwards, in his essay entitled "Christian Knowledge," can be very helpful here. He writes, "Christians should not always remain babes, but should grow in christian [*sic*] knowledge; and leaving the food of babes, they should learn to digest strong meat."[21] His concern is that Christians should grow in their ability to understand "divine things," that is, things that particularly pertain to the life of faith. Edwards calls for serious, determined action in this area. He writes:

> The faculty by which we are chiefly distinguished from the brutes, is the faculty of understanding. It follows, then, that we should make it our chief business to improve this faculty, and should by no means prosecute it as a business by the bye.[22]

He offers seven very helpful suggestions on how we may "prosecute" this business.

1. Be assiduous in reading the Holy Scriptures.
2. Content not yourselves with only a cursory reading, without regarding the sense.
3. Procure, and diligently use, other books which may help you to grow in this knowledge.
4. Improve conversation with others to this end.
5. Seek not to grow in knowledge chiefly for the sake of applause, and to enable you to dispute with others; but seek it for the benefit of your souls, and in order to practice.
6. Seek to God, that he would direct you, and bless you in this pursuit after knowledge.
7. Practise according to what knowledge you have.[23]

As we grow in our ability to understand divine things and put them to use, we find that our store of light for analyzing popular culture from a kingdom perspective has grown brighter and is more readily available for the task of taking every thought captive for Christ.

Thus fortified intellectually, with a mind that is being perfected to understand the forms of popular culture and to analyze them from the perspective of a biblical worldview, we shall be much better prepared to gain the benefit of popular culture without being overwhelmed by it. Our prayers will be enriched and our minds will be sharpened to carry out the task of controlling the kudzu of popular culture that daily confronts us.

Approaching Popular Culture Purposefully

We must strive to make certain that our approach to popular culture is purposeful. As we have seen, Christians are a people with a mission, called to embody, proclaim, and advance the kingdom of God and His righteousness. Everything we do must be seen in the light of this supreme calling, and we must do nothing that does not contribute to our realizing this purpose.

What will this require of us? First, it means that we may no longer adopt a merely passive approach to popular culture. We must get beyond the mindless playing of popular songs in our cars as mere background music. Channel-surfing the television for whatever most titillates us must be an extremely low priority in the kingdom calling of the Christian. We must rethink our approach to going to films and renting videos merely for an evening's diversion. Our involvement in various sports and recreations must be carefully reevaluated. Passively participating in popular culture is like walking through an open field without regard for the many "hitchhiking" seeds that will inevitably stick to our clothing. The messages and priorities of popular culture will cling and adhere to us whether we are attentive to them or not. Whether we notice them enough to pick them off will be determined by whether or not we are paying careful attention.

Instead, let us carefully consider the use we make of popular culture, asking such questions as, Why am I indulging in this form at this time? What do I hope to learn from this activity? How will this help me to grow as a Christian or to perfect my Christian thinking about the world? How will I use this encounter with popular culture to advance the cause of Christ and His kingdom? Are there better things that I might do with my time? Such questions can help to ensure that our minds are properly geared up for the encounter with popular culture, and that we are not being seduced to embrace views or positions that are at odds with our kingdom calling.

In addition, we must become more intentional about our involvement with popular culture. We must think carefully about our participation in it, and even plan the use of our time with popular culture so as to grow in the wisdom of the Lord. Such "numbering our days"—thinking carefully about how we will use our time in the engagement with popular culture—will be more likely to lead us to the heart of wisdom that Moses sought in Psalm 90:12. We can only redeem the time allotted to us by the Lord if we think in advance about how we plan to use it, and if we are careful and circumspect as we are spending our time, that it might be wisely invested for the righteousness of Christ and His kingdom.

Finally, we must resolve to become better students of popular culture, beginning with those forms that most enthrall us. The study of popular culture can yield much in the way of a greater knowledge of and love for the Lord, as we shall argue in the next chapter. As we participate in His gifts to others, we can celebrate His goodness, rejoice in His beauty, and grow in His grace. But this will require greater understanding of the forms of popular culture and those who employ them. In my own case, for example, my appreciation of contemporary Celtic music, and the many gifts of God that go into its production, has been greatly enriched by taking the time to read and become familiar with its history, as well as the various forms it takes and the groups who play it. Now, as I put on a CD of Celtic music, I am seeking ways to understand the concerns of others, and to appreciate the gifts that God has given them in making those concerns known. Since a certain legitimacy attaches to almost every form of popular culture, there is plenty of room for us to explore existing interests, learn about those of others, and develop new ones as we prepare continuously for our engagement with this inescapable cultural presence.

Approaching Popular Culture Critically

It goes without saying that this aspect of a kingdom approach to popular culture will be impossible without the previous three. If, in approaching popular culture prayerfully, intelligently, and purposefully, we are concerned about our own motives in such engagements, in approaching it critically we are interested in the motives of those who produce and sponsor it. We want to discover their concerns, to ferret out the presuppositions that guide their thinking, and to analyze the various messages they send.

We have previously observed that popular culture is above all motivated by the bottom line. At the end of the day, money seems to be what drives the producers and promoters of popular culture. But money certainly is not all. Other motivations and concerns come into play as well. All of these are worthy of our attention, and some may even be worthy of our emulation. Self-expression, environmental concern, love that is more than merely erotic, correcting social injustice, the celebration of simple *joie de vivre,* the beauty and mystery of the created world, the humor of everyday life, and the trials and heroism of ordinary people—all these and more have found their way into the various forms of popular culture. We might expect to benefit from being exposed to some of these concerns, even though they may be strictly secondary in the various forms we encounter.

The thoroughness and doggedness, for example, of crime scene investigators, as dramatized in the television series *CSI,* can be an encouragement to all of us to do our work with care and excellence. Steve Irwin—the "Crocodile Hunter"—manifests a love for the animals he handles, and it is a rebuke to all of us who take the creation for granted each day. The music of the early Bob Dylan and Paul Simon can give us insight into the unrest and aspirations of an entire generation, and should lead us to weep for the way their dream of a new society has become a moral nightmare in our day.[24] Even the cleverness of advertisers can give us insights into what motivates our contemporaries in the pursuit of their dreams.

As we reflect on such concerns, and the many others that motivate popular culture, we might well benefit from thinking about what motivates us in our daily activities. Is all we do driven by mere self-interest, or are we able to nurture a concern for things that are wholly unrelated to the business of making a living? Further, we will discover concerns that should be matters of concern to us. The celebration of violence and raw sexuality which features large in some rap music, the exaltation of self above team by many professional athletes, and the use of popular culture to undermine established values should raise red flags in our minds. How are such concerns to be understood and responded to in our postmodern society? They should lead us to a more purposeful approach to our own involvement in popular culture.

Behind all these concerns are presuppositions—ideas and convictions that are, in the end, faith commitments, guiding all thinking and acting in the world. For example, I am alternately grieved and offended by the constant casual references in the many animal programs now available on cable channels to evolution as the underlying presupposition of all our understanding of the natural world. The ease with which the presupposition that homosexuality is a valid alternative lifestyle has established itself in the mainstream media should be greeted with sadness, if not alarm, as should the presupposition that sex without marriage is a settled norm in our society. The subtle and not-so-subtle ways that television and films debunk the role of religion in society reveal a presupposition of antisupernaturalism, which helps to explain why the church has become so marginal in our day.

By looking critically at the various forms of popular culture that confront us each day, we can ask questions about the underlying convictions–the presuppositions–that drive the producers and promoters of our cultural kudzu. What is their understanding of the notions of beauty, goodness, and truth? In their thinking, what constitutes the good life? How may we attain that ideal? What really matters in life, and what should be left behind or eliminated? Asking such questions will help us to discern the messages that the various forms of popular culture thrust upon us day by day.

The messages of popular culture bear powerfully on the people of our society. Anyone who has ever driven south from Lake Okeechobee on the Florida Turnpike will soon become aware of a curious phenomenon: all the trees on both sides of the road bend toward the Florida Everglades. This is because they are continually exposed to a subtle, unremitting sea breeze that wafts in from the Gold Coast, intercepts the trees in their normal path of growth toward the sun, and bends them in toward the Everglades. The messages of popular culture are like that. Wafting over us every day and from every angle, they subtly influence us by their distinctive messages, bending us away from the truth of God and His Word and contributing to our growth in ways that are contrary to His plan. It ill behooves us in the kingdom of God to be unmindful of these subtle but powerful messages.

We have already hinted at some of those messages: mere sensuality, materialism, the denigration of spiritual and religious things, absolute relativism, and a live-for-the-moment mentality. These are the ideas that fill the minds and determine the hopes of many of our contemporaries. Our witness to them, and our ability to live distinctive lives before them, will be greatly impeded if we fail to understand these messages, or if they so overwhelm us that our lives prove to be no different from theirs. A critical approach to popular culture can equip us to consider the concerns, discern the presuppositions, and respond to the messages that are shaping the lives of millions of our contemporaries, and help us avoid being overwhelmed by the kudzu of popular culture.

Approaching Popular Culture Dialogically

The idea of dialogue assumes interaction between interested parties on a common theme, and dialogue must play an important role in our engagement with popular culture. We are not sufficient on our own either to understand all the forms of popular culture or to formulate a proper approach to them. We will benefit, therefore, from interacting with others on this aspect of our kingdom calling.

We need to dialogue first of all with the creators and proponents of popular culture by allowing them to speak to us in their own words about their concerns and the products of their hands. As has already been suggested, we can do this through reading and study, as well as through careful and critical participation in the forms of popular culture. But we will also benefit from firsthand discussion with those who are immersed in the popular culture of the day. There are several ways in which we can do this, but one of the most fruitful is in the context of a discussion group. Many local bookstores, especially the larger chains, sponsor such groups. They are easy enough to join, and participating in them will provide plenty of opportunity to hear how others respond to the forms of popular culture, and to inquire as to why they find them particularly pleasurable. These groups may not be directly tied to popular culture; they may focus on reading and discussing poetry, philosophy, a current best seller, or some classic. However, in any of these settings one might expect to be able to inject questions about contemporary popular culture and receive enlightening responses from the participants.

Another way to become involved in this kind of dialogue is through courses at local colleges or community colleges, either in regular courses of study (which can be audited) or through continuing education courses. Secure a catalog or bulletin and study it carefully. Normally it will not be difficult to find a course that will allow you to interact with others who are engaged in some of the forms of popular culture. There will be some cost, but auditing and continuing education fees are not exorbitant, and you should regard them as an investment for the kingdom.

You can also begin your own group, inviting colleagues at work, neighbors, and others who are immersed in the popular culture to join you for discussion. Choose books, TV programs, films, or music as a subject, or rotate through all of them over time. A sports bar is also a good setting for meeting with others to discuss the world of intercollegiate and professional athletics, although one must be particularly careful about one's demeanor in such a context.[25] There will also be plenty of opportunities for informal discussions with friends and colleagues on the job, at the health club, or in other kinds of gatherings. Like Paul in Athens,[26] we should see these as learning opportunities and listen carefully to others as they explain what they like about, and what they find meaningful in, the various forms of popular culture in which they are involved.

But we will also benefit from gathering with other Christians to discuss such matters. Here again, a discussion group, a Bible study, or a Sunday school class can be helpful. You might study a Christian book on this subject—by Ken Myers, William D. Romanowski, Robert K. Johnston, Jeremy Begbie, or someone else—or listen to an edition of *Mars Hill Journal* and discuss it together. I have often introduced forms of popular culture into a teaching setting and invited the members of my class to interact with their concerns and messages, and I have always found these to lead to much fruitful discussion. On occasion, after viewing a video with family or friends, my wife Susie and I will encourage discussion of what we have seen, and think aloud together about how we might respond to the messages of popular culture we have seen. My son Kevin and I have at times read books together and benefited from one another's insights into the author's purposes and concerns.

However we accomplish it, some dialogue with others should play a crucial role in our approach to popular culture. In such a setting, where iron sharpens iron,[27] we will find stimulation, insights, and mutual encouragement to nurture a proper kingdom response to the forms of popular culture that we encounter each day.

Approaching Popular Culture Redemptively

The various aspects of a kingdom approach to popular culture that we have examined thus far are preparatory to enabling us to control the cultural kudzu from a kingdom perspective. We want to gain whatever benefit popular culture might have for us (as we shall see in the next chapter), while keeping up our guard against being so overwhelmed by the forms of popular culture that our distinctiveness as Christians begins to be obscured. We are called to be the salt of the earth, preserving what is good and useful; the light of the world, leading the way to truth and righteousness; and the leaven of grace in a sin-soaked world. Thus, the end of our prayers, thoughtful interactions, purposeful engagements, critical assessments, and dialogues on the forms of popular culture must be the redeeming and reconciling work to which we have been called as citizens of God's kingdom.

This will have at least three aspects to it.

Our own redemption. Our first concern must be our own further redemption. Each of us will discover that our approach to popular culture, once we have prayerfully and critically weighed it in the balance, will be found wanting. We will identify attitudes that are unbecoming, pleasures that are purely selfish, cultural activities that are a waste of precious kingdom time, and areas of indifference to popular culture that do not serve us well in reaching out to our friends and neighbors. We must resolve to redeem the time of our lives, to be renewed in the spirit of our minds, to guard our hearts, and to dedicate our lives to seeking first the kingdom of God and His righteousness in all we do. As we pray, think, and dialogue about the forms of popular culture in which we are currently engaged, let us be prepared to be rebuked by the Lord, corrected by Christian friends, humbled by the sincerity of the lost and touched by the darkness that blinds them, and opened up to new ways of thinking about what is truly pleasing to God. Let us commit our way to the Lord, even in the use we make of popular culture, so that He might direct our feet in paths of beauty, goodness, and truth.[28] In this area, as in all other areas of our lives, we must remember that God is at work within us, renewing our hearts and minds and revitalizing our will to love Him and our neighbors more perfectly. We must be equally dedicated to working out our salvation with a view to doing all things for the glory and pleasure of God.[29]

The redemption of our witness. We must give ourselves to the redemption of our witness for the Lord. Paul encourages us to be all things to all people, in order that by all means we might win some.[30] It takes a wise person to be a winner of souls, and part of the wisdom we need for communicating effectively will come from understanding and using the forms of popular culture as part of our witness for Christ.[31] The often cited example of Paul in Athens (Acts 17) is worth reviewing here. As he went about the city and dialogued with people in various settings, Paul came to understand what occupied their minds and filled their hearts. What he observed disturbed him greatly. When he began to preach to them, he did not regale them with biblical texts or theological premises; rather, having first complimented them for their zeal in spiritual matters, he addressed the crowds in language familiar to them, quoting from their cultural sources and using these to illustrate truths that he wished to make known. He did not neglect to proclaim Jesus, but he built a bridge of cultural identification with them, over which he marched the great truths of the gospel for their review. His example and teaching must be instructive for us as well, as we seek grace to renew and redeem our witness for Christ amid the kudzu of American popular culture.

The redemption of popular culture. Finally, we must devote ourselves to the redemption of popular culture in kingdom expressions. The forms of popular culture, as most forms of culture, have a certain inherent validity, given where they derive from and given that they are the products of those who are the image-bearers of God. This does not mean that we will find all those forms agreeable or pleasurable. Nor do I intend to sanction all the particular expressions of popular culture as beautiful, good, or true *per se.* I may not like rap music, and I may have concluded that some rap music is more an instrument of the devil than a useful cultural form. However, my opinions and conclusions do not negate the possibility of rap music being used as an instrument of kingdom progress. Christian musicians such as Carmen and the group D. C. Talk have, I think, clearly demonstrated the potential of rap for expressing kingdom concerns and energizing the hearts of God's people for greater love for Him and for their neighbors. My point is simply that, as citizens of the kingdom of God, we must examine every possible avenue of expression for that kingdom reality, taking every thought and every cultural form captive to make it obedient to Christ.

Here, of course, many Christians are already actively engaged in laying hold of various forms of popular culture for the purposes of Christ's kingdom. Contemporary Christian music, specifically Christian programming on radio and television, and Christian novels and films are all valid attempts to fulfill this redemptive aspect of our approach to popular culture. I will be the first to admit that much of our work thus far has been pioneering and is, as we might expect at this early stage, exploratory, simplistic, and not likely to last. But those involved in the work of redeeming popular culture—both as producers and consumers—should be encouraged, and we should join them in doing what we can to promote excellence in our kingdom labors in this area.

In my own case, for example, this means coming to terms with contemporary Christian music, which I have never liked, because of its primarily pietistic and merely imitative forms. My friend Steven Wright has encouraged me over the years not to despair and to keep listening. Now a few musicians—Steven Curtis Chapman and Phil Keaggy, in particular—have begun to impress me with their masterful compositions. In many of their works, I hear originality: themes that go beyond your basic "me 'n' Jesus" motif, and lyrics that are at times witty and delightful, at other times powerful and prophetic. I try to encourage such musicians by buying their albums, sharing them with others, talking about their music, and writing about them.

Similarly, each of us must seek to contribute to the work of reclaiming popular culture for the purposes of Christ and His kingdom. By supporting and dialoguing with Christian pop artists, being selective in our participation in Christian pop culture, and working to improve our understanding and use of this growing phenomenon, we can help to ensure that the forms of popular culture that emerge from within the Christian community will play a significant role in advancing the kingdom of Christ.

Salt, Light, and Yeast

As new creatures in Christ, we are called to exert a kingdom presence in the world, to impact everything we touch with the newness of Christ—invading, pervading, and transforming all of life with the renewing grace and truth of God. This is true of our involvement with popular culture as well. We may expect to discover beauty, goodness, and truth in that kudzu, and we can learn to put it to good use for the cause of Christ. As we prayerfully, intelligently, purposefully, critically, dialogically, and redemptively enter the realm of popular culture, we can expect the Lord to bless our involvement and to use us more effectively for His purposes in making all things new and reconciling the world to our reigning and returning King.

Study Questions

1. Think about Jesus' referring to His followers as salt, light, and yeast. What do these images suggest about the role of Christians in the popular culture?
2. Take each of the six aspects of a kingdom approach to popular culture discussed in this chapter (and listed below) and rate yourself on a scale of 1 to 10 as to where you presently stand with each of them. Let 10 be the highest rating. Overall, how would you rate your current approach to popular culture? Is it more kingdomlike or more individualistic?
   Prayerfully
   Intelligently
   Purposefully
   Critically
   Dialogically
   Redemptively
3. What would keep you from taking more of a kingdom approach to popular culture? Should you allow this to stand in your way? How might you overcome this obstacle?
4. Review the goals you established for this study back at the end of chapter 1. Are you making any progress? In what ways? Have any new goals been suggested to you?

5. The final chapter deals with expectations—in particular, how we may hope to benefit from taking a kingdom approach to popular culture. In preparation for that chapter, do some thinking about this on your own. How would you like to benefit from taking more of a kingdom approach to popular culture in your own life?

Six

Moments of Transcendence

Christian theology insists that humans made in God's image cannot but create works which communicate beyond the immediate and "internal" sensations they stimulate. Popular culture, that is to say, can have its moments of transcendence.
—GRAHAM CRAY[1]

The works of the LORD are great, sought out of all them that have pleasure therein.
—PSALM 111:2

Like everyone else, we expect our involvement with popular culture to bring us a certain amount of pleasure. We want to laugh, to be entertained or excited, to have a good time with friends, or just to relax and escape the cares and concerns of the world. There is nothing inherently wrong with such goals. As we have seen, God Himself took pleasure in the things He made, and He has made us in His image, creatures able to enjoy and take pleasure in things. The kudzu of popular culture thrives on the need we all have for pleasure. And there is much of beauty, goodness, and truth to be discovered and enjoyed in the forms of popular culture.

The problem is that contemporary popular culture, with its emphasis on individual taste, entices us to seek pleasures that are not consistent with the divine pleasure, to indulge for merely sensual or selfish ends, and to lust for things that are out of accord with our kingdom calling. All too often, the result is that the citizens of the kingdom fall into the decadence that popular culture nourishes, "the erosion of character, the spoiling of innocent pleasures, and the cheapening of life itself that often accompany modern popular culture,"[2] as Ken Myers puts it.

Does this mean that we are better off staying away from popular culture? Anyone who has read this far will know that my answer to that is no, not in the least. There have been times, however, when that has been my chosen course. For a while, disgusted with myself because of the easy way I deferred to popular culture as my avocation of choice, I resolved to listen to nothing but classical or Christian music. I refused to watch anything on television except news programs. I even gave up all active interest in sports, both playing and watching them. I wanted to outdo the Puritans in my separation from the kudzu of contemporary pop culture. I'm convinced now, however, that these were unwise courses of action. I missed a great deal of beauty, lost opportunities to experience the goodness of God, failed in important ways to understand how His truth applied to life in a postmodern society, allowed my tastes to grow stale, and settled into a narrow and not very efficient mode of seeking the kingdom of God and His righteousness. I have found it much more rewarding to rediscover that popular culture can be a rich resource for knowing God, enjoying Him more fully, and serving Him more faithfully in my particular calling.

The works of popular culture are, in many ways, if only indirectly, works of God Himself. As we have seen, His image in people, prompting the use of His gifts in the sustaining power of His Spirit, yields the products and forms of popular culture. And, while the sinful hearts, minds, and hands of men leave their stains and blots, and often render the works of their minds and hands wholly displeasing to the Lord, the forms of popular culture can still tell us much about God and about our contemporaries. Therefore, we should learn to delight in them according to our kingdom convictions, as we work hard to judge righteously and actively seek the benefits that they might hold for us.

But what should we expect from our involvement in popular culture? To the extent that we are committed to a *kingdom* approach to popular culture—such as I have discussed thus far—we may expect to be greatly blessed and more wondrously used of God in seeing His kingdom come on earth as it is in heaven. There are moments of glorious transcendence to be experienced in our involvement with popular culture. When we get beyond ourselves, we begin to see into the hearts and hopes of our contemporaries, grow in our ability to talk with them about the love of God, are moved with the experience of God's mercy and lovingkindness, and come to know, love, and delight in Him more and more.

In this final chapter, I want to outline five goals for taking a kingdom approach to popular culture that can guide our effort to control this kudzu, as we seek to gain its benefit without allowing ourselves to be overcome by it. A kingdom approach to popular culture can help us to achieve better understanding of our times and the people with whom we have to do, better communications with them, better recreating for our own pleasure and enrichment, better celebrating of God and His goodness, and better culture overall.

Better Understanding

The record of the achievements of David's "mighty men" is impressive, to say the least.[3] Here we find a catalog of heroic deeds, astonishing exploits, and noble conquests in the name of the Lord. Equally impressive is the register of the armies of Israel that constituted the fighting forces of David.[4] Tribe by tribe, they are described as men of war, mighty men who maintained their allegiance through all the king's trials and struggles, men of valor, famous men in their fathers' households, men who could quickly and efficiently assemble for battle and wield all kinds of weapons. These are all described as having perfect hearts and a single-mindedness in the cause of their king. That was an impressive array of supporters to lead into battle year after year!

Among these mighty men of David is one very curious listing: the sons of Issachar. Of them it is said simply that they understood the times and knew what Israel needed to do. Perhaps they were intelligence analysts, war planners, and so forth. These were men trained to understand their foes, calculate their strengths and weaknesses, keep track of their movements and of the various alliances that were being made against Israel, and consider the best ways of defending the nation against aggression. Without them, all those other mighty men and armies would have been of little use. Someone among the mighty men needed to study the enemy carefully, so that they could assess their capabilities, anticipate their movements, and make plans for how to confront and overcome them. This was the task of the sons of Issachar, who were mighty men indeed.

This is likewise part of our task in the battle to control the kudzu of popular culture, as I have already argued, and part of what we may hope to realize as we adopt a kingdom approach to popular culture. As William D. Romanowski has observed, “While there is much in popular culture that is mindless and trivial, the popular arts do have the capacity to provoke serious reflection on our lives and our society.”[5] Popular culture can yield important insights into the contemporary world, enabling us better to understand the times and discern how best to do the work of the kingdom in our own day. The better we understand the times, as represented in the various forms of popular culture, the greater will be our ability to see both the positive aspects of popular culture and the dangers inherent in it, and to develop effective strategies for benefiting from the one and guarding against being overwhelmed by the other.

Becoming familiar with the various forms of popular culture from a kingdom point of view can help us to grow in understanding in at least three ways.

Evaluating our own tastes. We can expect to gain a better assessment of our own tastes, of the particular kinds of pleasure we derive from popular culture. We can expect to discover areas in which our tastes are rooted in the delights of the flesh, in lust, greed, covetousness, and the idle pleasures of the natural man. Let's be honest about what we learn here, and resolve to overcome such pleasures before they overwhelm us and to work on shaping our tastes in a more godly direction.

But we can also expect to find that God has put in our hearts a wholesome ability to delight in things that are excellent—all the different forms of popular culture that are true, noble, pure, lovely, and of good report—virtuous and praiseworthy lyrics, melodies, plots, and accomplishments.[6] For these we can give God thanks and praise, and train our minds to discover what they reveal to us about Him. We can search out such excellencies in other forms of popular culture, thus increasing our store of knowledge, our ability to appreciate the gifts of God, and our reasons to thank and praise Him throughout the day. Careful consideration of the forms of popular culture from a kingdom perspective will aid us in training our affections, girding up our minds for action, and deepening our walk with the Lord.

Loving the lost. We can expect that a kingdom approach to understanding the forms of popular culture will enable us to grow in compassion for the lost. As we study their use of popular culture, we will discover that many of them are like sheep without a shepherd, desperately looking for something more meaningful and lasting than the postmodern miasma in which they are mired. Rather than begrudge them their success or despise them in their confusion, we will find our hearts moved to reach out to them in new and more effective ways.[7] We must remember that our heavenly Father loved the world in all its lostness, loved it so much that He gave His only begotten Son to rescue His elect from the darkness of unbelief and bring them into the kingdom of glorious light and truth. As He, understanding our desperate condition and deep need, adopted the forms of our existence to make Himself known to us, so we, understanding the forms of popular culture in which our contemporaries are immersed, and having compassion for them, will be in a better position to reach them with the gospel of Jesus Christ and the hope of His kingdom.[8]

Understanding postmodern people. Understanding the forms of popular culture will help us to understand the vain hopes that captivate postmodern people, the messages to which they cling and which they eagerly foist upon the rest of our culture and society. Without such an understanding, we run the risk of becoming like the foolish Galatians, who uncritically embraced half-truths and were in danger of apostatizing from the faith of Christ.[9] Romanowski notes, "Cultural activity reveals people's deep-seated beliefs and convictions about God, the meaning and purpose of life, and the nature of the universe."[10] Many of those convictions are expressed in messages that deny or otherwise oppose central truths of Scripture. And since these messages are subtly and pleasurably packaged, they can easily entice unwary recipients to embrace false ideas in all these areas. By adopting a kingdom approach to popular culture, we will be better able to discern the false winds of doctrine that waft across our path and to prepare ourselves—heart, mind, and life—to resist them as we strain to grow toward the light of Christ.[11]

The followers of Christ are to be renewed in the spirit of their mind and to resist the world's attempts to mold them after its own image.[12] Only by consciously endeavoring to understand and approach the forms of popular culture from a decidedly kingdom perspective will we be able to manage this important task and realize this critical objective.

Better Communications

Taking a kingdom approach to popular culture will equip us to communicate better with the people to whom we have been sent as ambassadors of Christ. No ambassador, entering a new field of endeavor, would neglect to understand and learn to use the protocols of the host culture. Failure to do so would result in one serious *faux pas* after another, needlessly strewing obstacles in the ambassador's path of service. In order to communicate effectively—and, thus, to serve effectively in Christ's kingdom—we must give ourselves to understanding the times in which we live, so that we might know how to do and say what is appropriate and what will enable us to represent our King and His concerns in clear and compelling terms. "All things are yours," the apostle reminds us, and we need to learn how to use them—including the forms of popular culture—in the pursuit of our kingdom calling.[13] "The task for Christians," Romanowski writes, "is to discover and employ the most effective roles and purposes for popular art in service of our neighbor."[14]

Again, in three ways we can expect that adopting a kingdom approach to popular culture will improve our ability to communicate in our postmodern times.

Communicating within the church. We will be better able to communicate with those in the body of Christ for whom popular culture is, if not their primary culture, at least an extremely important one. I have seen this on many occasions. Once, after a morning service in which guitars had been used to lead the congregation in praise songs, I was making my way back to the pulpit to retrieve my Bible and sermon notes. One of the young men of our congregation was standing with his back to me, playing something on one of the guitars. As I approached, I discerned the familiar opening riff of Jim Morrison's "Love Me Two Times, Baby." I crept quietly up behind the young man, and at just the right moment, sang softly over his shoulder, "Love me two times, baby; love me twice today." He turned quickly around, with a look of astonishment on his face, and said, "Do *you* know that song?" I answered that I did, and that I had seen The Doors in concert while in college. A brief conversation ensued about the merits of their music, but, more importantly, a friendship began with Karl Mischke, which has continued to this day.

Recently I was teaching a seminar on evangelism at a

church in northern Virginia. During one of the sessions, I was explaining the particular challenges of making the good news of Jesus known in a postmodern society. I was trying to illustrate the presuppositions and convictions of postmodernism to a very interested congregation, and used the film *Fight Club* as an organizing motif. Later that afternoon, after dinner at the home of one of the families, the oldest son, just getting ready to begin college, came up to me and said, "I thought that was so cool the way you used *Fight Club* to help us understand postmodernism. I was struggling to stay with you up to that point, but when you talked about that film, everything just seemed to fall into place."

Many members of the Christian community, especially young people, are steeped in the forms of popular culture. We run the risk of failing to communicate with them if we ignore or merely condemn that which plays such a large role in their lives. But we can expect to find many new avenues of communication opening up with them if we will adopt a kingdom approach to popular culture and begin incorporating our observations into our conversations with those who, like us, have been called to reach our postmodern generation with the good news of Christ and His kingdom.

Communicating with the world. We can expect that taking a kingdom approach to popular culture will equip us to communicate more effectively with our lost contemporaries. One way I have seen this is in the use of sports as an outreach activity of the local church and a bridge for personal evangelism. The church in which I serve has a large and diversified sports ministry as part of its missions effort. Butch Garman heads this program, which is among the most effective activities we have in reaching out to the lost in our community. Many unchurched families enroll their children in sports leagues and camps led by members of our church. Not only are they given excellent instruction in sports technique, and opportunities to play sports in a wholesome and supportive environment, but they also hear the gospel during team devotions and see it in the lives of coaches, team members, and parents. Our sports ministry also assembles teams for mission trips to other parts of the world, taking Christian athletes to reach out to sports enthusiasts of different cultures, using the common language of sports as a vehicle for proclaiming and exemplifying the good news of Christ and His kingdom.[15]

Many believers have found that sports provide an effective bridge for building relationships and sharing the gospel. My friend Charlie Wagner is a zealous supporter of Baltimore professional sports. He knows the Orioles and Ravens inside out, and talks enthusiastically with his colleagues at work about them, working hard to build relationships with them and to earn the right to share the more important and more exciting news of Christ. He participates in sports clubs and is active on a soccer team, all of which he does primarily as an arena for sharing the gospel with friends. Sports used to be an all-consuming passion for Charlie; now they are just one more tool in his growing kit for reaching lost persons for Christ.

For a time in college, I was a member of a singing group sponsored by the Fellowship of Christian Athletes. On many occasions, we traveled to some church or high school in Missouri, singing and speaking about our experiences as members of the Missouri football team and testifying to the saving love of Christ. We played mostly "secular" songs—at that time, folk and folk rock—but used the lyrics of those songs as part of our testimonies and presentations as we shared the gospel with the kids. We never failed to have the rapt attention of those who had come to hear us sing and speak.

Certain "crossover" artists among contemporary Christian musicians, such as Michael W. Smith, have also made conscious attempts to invest their success as pop artists in bringing the gospel to the lost. If they can use their songs to reach out in the name of Christ, so can we. The lyrics, melodies, and other forms of Christian popular culture can provide useful sources of dialogue within which to explore higher and more lasting things. As we learn to employ these forms, as well as those of the secular pop culture, from a kingdom perspective, in which we are gaining a better understanding of the concerns of our contemporaries, we will find that our ability to communicate with them is being greatly enhanced.

Communicating with God. We can expect to communicate better with God. Shallowness in prayer is an experience shared by many evangelicals. Sometimes we're just at a loss for words. We may feel reluctant to talk to God about things that strike us as simply too mundane. Or we don't know how to pray for some lost friend or neighbor. By growing in a kingdom approach to popular culture, examining our own tastes, and learning about the cultural interests of those around us, we will discover much more interesting and relevant matter to bring before the throne of grace. We will come to appreciate just how much God *is* interested in every aspect of our lives, and we will find new reasons to give Him abundant praise and thanks. We will seek His wisdom in new and more specific ways, call upon Him with clearer focus to keep us through temptation, and cry out to Him to help us grow in being pleasing to Him. Our conversations with God will become more personal and, frankly, more interesting, as we bring to His attention those aspects of contemporary popular culture that we are seeking to engage from a kingdom perspective.

Surely such improved communications are worth the effort! To be able to be more at one with other believers, to speak with more interest and enthusiasm to the lost, and to communicate more effectively with our heavenly Father are goals that every believer should be seeking. We can realize these goals more effectively if we will devote ourselves to a kingdom approach to popular culture.

Better Recreating

Certainly there is a place for rest and recreation in our lives as citizens of God's kingdom. Even the Lord Jesus seemed to imply as much.[16] Bodily exercise and all the other diversions of popular culture may be of only a little profit, but that profit can be useful in our service to the Lord.[17] Especially if we can learn to use our diversions and avocations as elements of our kingdom callings, we might expect to benefit richly from them, as Jonathan Edwards advised:

> So we ought to subordinate all our other business, and all our temporal enjoyments, to this affair of travelling to heaven. Thus we should eat and drink and clothe ourselves and improve our conversation and enjoyment of friends. And whatever business we are setting about, whatever design we are engaging in, we should inquire with ourselves, whether this business or undertaking will forward our way to heaven![18]

I'm not much of a baseball fan, but I do enjoy watching a game from time to time, especially in person. I remember the first time I walked into Camden Yards in Baltimore. I had never seen a lovelier ballpark. The beautiful architecture, the lush grass, the antique lettering all around, and all the sights, sounds, and smells made me give thanks to God for the many wondrous gifts and diversions He affords us. Baseball can be such a wonderful combination of strategy, skill, and opportunism, all emerging from the mix of talents, timing, and momentum that any inning might generate, often in unexpected and exciting ways. With a little effort, we can learn to see baseball—and other forms of sports—as beneficial to our kingdom calling to know the Lord and serve Him.

I especially like watching a game with my son Kevin, who, besides loving the Lord, knows baseball. He sees things developing that I would never have anticipated, even to the point of explaining how a pitcher might throw to a particular batter. Batting averages, player tendencies, pitching records, and so forth trickle off his lips like Scripture quotes from a preacher. Baseball is a very intellectual game for Kevin, because he has taken the time from a busy schedule of work and family to understand it well. My experience of a baseball game is greatly enriched just by being with him, whether at the Yard or in front of a TV set. His commentary, insights, and speculations help me to appreciate the game more fully. I find watching baseball not only much more enjoyable when I'm watching it with Kevin, but I am more likely at such times to marvel at the good gifts of God to people, and to wonder at Him and rejoice in thanksgiving at His manifest goodness.

The same can be true of other types of involvement in sports. On one occasion, when Susie and I were visiting our daughter Kristy and her family, we attended a gymnastics program in which our grandchildren were participating and Kristy was coaching. How it pleased me to see the way she interacted with those two- and three-year-old kids! She loved and encouraged them, showed them how to do each exercise to the best of their ability, and spoke affirmingly to them, no matter how well or how poorly they performed! But even more than that, there was an evident joy in her face and a spring in her step—even though she was eight months pregnant—that was lacking in many of her fellow coaches. Kristy, a former gymnast herself, had taken the time to understand each exercise and how it was to be done, and to learn each child's name and ability, and she seemed to be having a great deal of fun. She was on a mission for Christ and His kingdom, and her ability to perform that mission, and to enjoy herself in the bargain, was greatly enhanced by her knowledge of the sport and of the little ones she had been called to serve.

What is true for our involvement in sports can be true for all the different forms of popular culture. The more consciously we approach them from a kingdom perspective, the more we will benefit from them. Recently I was encouraged by my friend, Robert Hodge, to take an interest in bluegrass music. Knowing that I played acoustic guitar and mountain dulcimer, Robert put me on to a local radio station and urged me to have a listen. I have begun paying careful attention to the words of bluegrass and doing some reading about it. It is surprising how much the lyrics of bluegrass music (I admit, more a form of regional than popular culture) represent a morality that is either overtly declarative of or, at least, not inconsistent with the interests of the kingdom. Moreover, I am pleasantly surprised at the high level of skill of bluegrass musicians. Now, every time I take up my guitar or dulcimer, I am reminded to thank God for these wonderful instruments and play them with greater delight than ever (albeit with far less skill than those I am coming to admire!).

The forms of popular culture provide many wonderful opportunities to delight in the Lord and the creations of His hand, for, as Robert K. Johnston observes, "If the Spirit is active in and through the human spirit, then the potential for the sacred is present across our human endeavor."[19] How much richer our participation in these activities can be when we learn to enter them with our kingdom calling in mind, and seek to use them for the glory and enjoyment of God.

Better Celebration

Our chief end in this life is to glorify God and enjoy Him forever, and we can expect to become more efficient at each of these as we work hard at taking a kingdom approach to the forms of popular culture that confront us.

In the first place, we cannot pursue a kingdom approach to popular culture without at the same time seeking the Lord more earnestly.[20] We are not interested in learning about popular culture for its own sake; rather, our objective is to discover the beauty, goodness, and truth of the Lord, to improve our own tastes, to be pleased with what pleases Him, and to prepare ourselves as His ambassadors to serve the interests of His kingdom. God is revealing things about Himself in the works of popular culture, but we have to look carefully to discern them, always laboring to assess the various forms before us in the light of God's Word. Can we see in the skills and products of pop artists the goodness of God, who gives such gifts to men? Can we learn more about how He wants us to think about Him, and about what is beautiful, good, and true? Can we discover more matter for our prayers, more depth to our worship, and more joy in our relationship with the Lord as a result of our kingdom involvement with popular culture? I believe we can, but only if we are involved within the context of those kingdom commitments that I discussed in previous chapters. Deeper immersion in popular culture for its own sake has no particular virtue; indeed, it can be harmful, as the kudzulike tendrils of this tenacious phenomenon work their way into our hearts, minds, and lives. But by approaching popular culture self-consciously, as ambassadors for Christ and His kingdom, as well as prayerfully, intelligently, purposefully, critically, dialogically, and redemptively, we may seek the hand of God in many of the forms of popular culture and learn more about this One who gives such wondrous gifts to men and sets them to seeking after Him.

Second, we can expect our kingdom approach to popular culture to lead us to take more wholesome and consistent delight in Him. The Scriptures call us to delight ourselves in the Lord, and to trust in Him at all times.[21] To delight in the Lord is to enjoy being in His presence, thinking about Him, communing with Him in prayer and silent meditation, and feeling our hearts fill with joy and love as we increase in knowledge of Him. It may be hard to imagine that the forms of popular culture can enhance our ability to delight in the Lord, but it is true. Consider, for example, how the lyrics of numerous psalms seem to have been adapted to popular songs of the day.[22] Something in those ancient forgotten melodies struck the psalm writers as providing just the right mood to enhance what they wanted to say about the Lord. They believed that using those tunes would enable God's people to celebrate Him with greater understanding and delight.

Similarly, many of the forms of popular culture, as they help us grow in our understanding of ourselves, our contemporaries, and the goodness of the Lord, can lead us to take more evident delight in Him, to rejoice in Him more frequently and more overtly, and to encourage others to join us in this as well. Beautiful melodies, the excellent execution of skills, and true messages can be found in popular culture. Who of us has not delighted in the songs of Carol King, Paul McCartney, or Sarah MacLaughlin? Who has not marveled at the acting skills of Jack Nicholson, Brad Pitt, or Holly Hunter? Who would disagree that messages of devotion to spouse, nation, and "traditional" morality can be found in the forms of popular culture? Sincere questions are being raised there, by people seeking something more than merely sensual and material gratification. All these things should lead us to see how vast is the store of God's grace, how rich is His wisdom, how abundant is His kindness, and how wondrous is His beauty. He enables people to accomplish such things and makes Himself known through the efforts, whether intentional or otherwise, even of those who do not honor Him. Like Paul making a similar observation before the Greeks on Mars Hill, we may delight in all the ways that God reveals Himself, and use our observations both to celebrate Him and to call our contemporaries to join us in this high privilege.

Finally, we can expect to celebrate God more consistently, thus moving closer to fulfilling our calling to pray without ceasing and to give thanks in everything.[23] Prayer is perhaps the most distinctive aspect of the Christian life. Among other things, prayer provides a context for deepening our relationship with the Lord and yielding our lives more completely to Him. Most Christians maintain particular times during the day when they come before the Lord in prayer. Using prayer lists or the Scriptures as their guides, they bring before the Lord their praise and thanks, personal requests, and intercessions for others as they seek His mercy and grace to help in times of need. Further, throughout the day we receive cues and summons from the Lord to come before Him—at meal times, when someone asks us to pray about a particular situation or need, when we are involved in a study group, or when some prayer need pops into our mind.

By paying more careful attention to the cues provided by the popular culture, we increase the opportunities of conversing with the Lord, reflecting on His goodness and beauty, praising Him for His gifts to people, celebrating His truth, and thanking Him for the little delights we enjoy every day. A kingdom approach to popular culture will make us more aware of such cues and lead us to reflect in prayer on how we should respond to God for what we encounter in the popular culture around us. Every song we hear, ad we read, game we enjoy, television program we watch, or other diversion can be a springboard to prayer, leading us to think out loud before the Lord about what we have seen or heard, and asking His Spirit to guide us as we express our response in prayer to Him. Such prayer can be an effective forge for hammering out our understanding of popular culture, developing proper tastes, and thinking about how to use the knowledge we are gaining in the service of our King.

Better Culture

Finally, we can expect that taking a kingdom approach to popular culture will make for better culture, for ourselves as well as for our contemporaries.

As our own tastes grow, enabling us to take pleasure in the kinds of things God takes pleasure in, and laying aside those that are merely sensual and self-indulgent, we should feel more confident that our involvement in popular culture has a definite kingdom purpose and is, therefore, not only beneficial to us and others, but honoring to God as well. We will begin to choose the forms of popular culture that give us such "holy pleasure" and will divest ourselves of those that incline us to decadence. We will find increasing strength to resist the temptations of popular culture and a growing ability to see the hand of God in the gifts of others and to praise Him accordingly. The choices of pop culture that we make will more and more reinforce our kingdom commitment and will, rather than tempt or draw us away from our calling as ambassadors of Christ, actually contribute to our realizing that calling more effectively day by day in all the ways I have discussed above.

Moreover, growing in a kingdom approach to popular culture should enable us to affect the cultural choices of others, thus (it might be hoped) raising the level and standards of culture in the society as a whole. Evangelicals have tried in vain to achieve this objective through various political ploys and other forms of pressure. I wonder if we might not find that we are more effective at influencing the cultural tastes of our contemporaries in more positive directions by taking the time to understand and talk with them about the forms of popular culture in which they are involved and by inviting them to consider those in which we take pleasure.

We should not neglect the power of the bottom line, the driving force of popular culture. As our cultural tastes improve and our choices change, our decisions on what to purchase and what to pass by may well have an impact on what the producers of popular culture determine to bring to the market. I rather suspect that if evangelical consumers would begin to make their cultural choices with more self-conscious kingdom priorities guarding their hearts, the effect of that on the forms of popular culture would be dramatic over time.

Finally, it is surely not too much to expect that growing in a kingdom approach to popular culture will encourage the development of a broader, more highly developed, and more potent Christian popular culture. I have already mentioned that I am encouraged by some of what I see in contemporary Christian music. Some. However, most of it seems to celebrate a rather gushy pietism and will appeal only to those who have already come to know the Lord (and whose tastes in popular music are not very refined). Christian television is a wasteland, populated by local spiritual warlords who employ questionable tactics to win the allegiance and support of an audience that has grown hardly at all over the past twenty years (and which consists mainly of those who already share the convictions of those they watch so faithfully). Christian radio is only a little better, while Christian film barely exists, except as a tool for evangelism or to sensationalize those end-times events concerning which our Lord said that it was "not for you to know."[24] Christian "romance novels" are, in my opinion, an embarrassment. The Christian print media—with some notable exceptions, such as *First Things*—is largely ignored by those outside the pale of evangelicalism. And those Christians who are endeavoring to serve the Lord within the popular culture—actors and actresses, writers, musicians, athletes, and so forth—have yet to demonstrate that their presence is leavening that culture in a less sensual, less narcissistic, and less hedonistic direction.

Apologists for the use of the forms of popular culture that evangelicals are currently making will argue that many souls are being won for the kingdom of Christ, and that this is the best and most effective use of popular culture. While it is no doubt true, as Romanowski observes, that these various forms and involvements in popular culture have resulted in some people coming to faith in Christ, I also agree with him when he warns against the danger of a narrow and eccentric use of popular culture for evangelistic purposes alone.

> Believing that the only reason to create popular art is for evangelism, Christians portray religion as a narrow aspect of life, instead of as a life orientation. But if Christ is Lord over all things, then the popular art that Christians produce should not only affirm but also demonstrate this profound belief in God's sovereign rule.[25]

If all of us in the evangelical community would begin to take a more decidedly kingdom approach to popular culture, might we not reasonably expect the Lord to bless the works of our hands, and to bring to light a broader, more impressive, and more potent evangelical popular culture? One that provoked our contemporaries to consider more carefully the claims of Christ? One that enabled them to see more readily the evidence of God's glory and that prompted them to seek Him more earnestly? Or one that at least compelled them to conform their own cultural activities to norms more in keeping with the kingdom interests of Christ?[26]

By taking a kingdom approach to our involvement with popular culture—as opposed to an unthinking, merely pleasure-oriented approach—we may expect to benefit in all these ways, achieving better understanding, better communications, better recreating, better celebration, and better culture. Continuing to approach popular culture merely from the perspective of what we like—what delights and makes us happy, gets us excited, causes us to laugh, or moves our spirits somehow—can be merely self-indulgent, opening the soil of our hearts and minds to the ever-eager tendrils of popular culture. When we approach popular culture this way, we run the risk of being taken captive by its presuppositions and messages, of being squeezed into the world's mold and forfeiting our kingdom distinctives, and of being overwhelmed by the kudzu of popular culture. But a kingdom approach to popular culture, besides being more interesting and exciting, can enable us to discover its benefits for our callings in the kingdom of Christ and can help us to be more effective as His servants in the post-modern world.

Study Questions

1. In which of the areas discussed in this chapter would you like to derive more benefit from your involvement in popular culture? What might that look like as you begin to realize that objective?
2. What progress have you made in realizing the goals you set for this study? Have any new goals been suggested to you along the way?
3. What's next for you? What will you do with what you have studied in this book? Can your current involvement in popular culture continue? Do you need to make some changes? In what ways?
4. Think of the people you know who are deeply immersed in the various forms of popular culture. How might your taking a kingdom approach to popular culture better prepare you to show them the love of Christ and to help them see something more of the reality of His kingdom? What will that require of you?
5. Below, make a list of five things you would like to begin praying about with regard to your involvement in popular culture. See if you can attach a promise of God's Word to each one of them. Then begin praying about them faithfully, asking the Lord to help you respond to the challenge of popular culture in a way that will benefit you the most and bring greater honor and glory to Him.

Notes

Introduction

1 Kenneth A. Myers, *All God's Children and Blue Suede Shoes* (Wheaton, Ill.: Crossway, 1989), xii.

2 See, for example, John Frow, *Cultural Studies and Cultural Value* (Oxford: Clarendon Press, 1995); Paul R. Gorman, *Left Intellectuals and Popular Culture in Twentieth-Century America* (Chapel Hill: University of North Carolina Press, 1996); John Storey, *Cultural Studies and the Study of Popular Culture* (Athens, Ga.: University of Georgia Press, 1996). See also the excellent approach to film analysis in Robert K. Johnston, *Reel Spirituality* (Grand Rapids: Baker, 2000).

3 As a literary example of this approach, see Simon Frith, *Performing Rites: On the Value of Popular Music* (Cambridge, Mass.: Harvard University Press, 1996).

4 Thomas S. Hibbs, *Shows About Nothing* (Dallas: Spence Publishing, 1999).

5 1 Chron. 12:32.

6 1 Thess. 5:21.

7 1 John 4:1-3.

8 Eph. 5:11.

9 2 Cor. 10:3-5.

10 Matt. 28:18-20; Gen. 1:26-28.

11 Jonathan Edwards, *The Religious Affections* (Edinburgh: Banner of Truth, 1986), 24.

12 Ibid., 25–26.

13 Cf. Frow, *Cultural Studies and Cultural Value,* 70–71; Storey, *Cultural Studies and the Study of Popular Culture,* 18–25.

14 John Fiske, "Popular Discrimination," in *Modernity and Mass Culture,* ed. James Naremore and Patrick Brantlinger (Bloomington: Indiana University Press, 1991), 108.

15 Cf. Frow, *Cultural Studies and Cultural Value,* 144ff.

16 Ibid., 145.

17 Daniel Taylor, *The Myth of Certainty* (Downers Grove, Ill.: InterVarsity Press, 1992), 21.

18 Frow, *Cultural Studies and Cultural Value,* 63–64.

19 Myers, *All God's Children and Blue Suede Shoes,* 30.

20 Matt. 6:33.

Chapter 1: Culture, Cultures, and Popular Culture

1 Edmund P. Clowney, *The Church* (Downers Grove, Ill.: InterVarsity Press, 1995), 179.

2 William D. Romanowski, *Pop Culture Wars* (Downers Grove, Ill.: InterVarsity Press, 1996), 82.

3 Jacques Barzun, *The Culture We Deserve* (Middletown, Conn.: Wesleyan University Press, 1989), 3.

4 John Storey, *Cultural Studies and the Study of Popular Culture* (Athens, Ga.: University of Georgia Press, 1996), 2.

5 Kenneth A. Myers, *All God's Children and Blue Suede Shoes* (Wheaton, Ill.: Crossway, 1989), 34.

6 Storey, *Cultural Studies and the Study of Popular Culture,* 3.

7 William D. Romanowski, *Eyes Wide Open: Looking for God in Popular Culture* (Grand Rapids: Brazos Press, 2001), 17.

8 Thomas S. Hibbs, *Shows About Nothing* (Dallas: Spence Publishing, 1999), 4.

9 John Frow, *Cultural Studies and Cultural Value* (Oxford: Clarendon Press, 1995), 82.

10 I'm reminded of a lyric from an Olivia Newton-John song of the early 1970s in which the singer, protesting the genuineness of her love, declared, "It's comin' from my heart and not my head."

11 Myers, *All God's Children and Blue Suede Shoes,* xiii.

12 Romanowski, *Pop Culture Wars,* 323.

13 Cf. Geoffrey Nowell-Smith, "On Kiri Te Kanawa, Judy Garland, and the Culture Industry," in *Modernity and Mass Culture,* ed. James Naremore and Patrick Brantlinger (Bloomington: Indiana University Press, 1991), 77.

14 Cf. Christopher Anderson, "Hollywood in the Home: TV and the End of the Studio System," in *Modernity and Mass Culture,* ed. James Naremore and Patrick Brantlinger, 83.

15 Graham Cray, "Through Popular Music: 'Wholly Holy'?" in *Beholding the Glory,* ed. Jeremy Begbie (Grand Rapids: Baker, 2000), 119.

16 Jacques Barzun, *From Dawn to Decadence: 500 Years of Western Cultural Life* (New York: HarperCollins, 2000), 11.

17 See, for example, Ken Myers's interview with Morris Berman on *Mars Hill Tape* 49.

Chapter 2: Popular Culture and Our Kingdom Calling

1 Edmund P. Clowney, *The Church* (Downers Grove, Ill.: InterVarsity Press, 1995), 207.

2 John 18:36.

3 Rom. 14:17.

4 1 Cor. 4:20.

5 2 Cor. 6:17.

6 1 John 2:15.

7 Matt. 28:18–20; 2 Cor. 5:17–19.

8 Eph. 1:18–23; Matt. 12:22–29.

9 1 Cor. 3:21–23.

10 2 Cor. 10:3–5.

11 Gen. 1:26–28; Ps. 8.

12 1 Cor. 10:31.

13 Clowney, *The Church,* 207, 176.

14 Ps. 24:1.

15 Herman Ridderbos, *The Coming of the Kingdom,* trans. H. de Jongste, ed. Raymond O. Zorn (Philadelphia: Presbyterian and Reformed, 1962), 19.

16 Clowney, *The Church,* 38.

17 For a more complete discussion of the kingdom of God and its relationship to the church, see my book *Living in God's Covenant* (Phillipsburg, N.J.: P&R Publishing, 2002).

18 Matt. 12:28; 1 Cor. 4:20; Acts 1:8.

19 Dan. 2:44–45.

20 Dan. 11:32–33; 12:3.

21 Gen. 1:26–28; 2:8–17.

22 2 Chron. 2:11ff.

23 Ps. 68:15–16.

24 1 Cor. 12.

25 William D. Romanowski, *Pop Culture Wars* (Downers Grove, Ill.: InterVarsity Press, 1996), 82.

26 Inagrace T. Dietterich, "A Particular People: Toward a Faithful and Effective Ecclesiology," in *Church Between Gospel and Culture,* ed. George R. Hunsberger and Craig Van Gelder (Grand Rapids: Eerdmans, 1996), 368.

27 Cf. Ps. 50.

28 Cf. Acts 4:32–37; 6:1–7; 11:27–30.

29 Cf. Gal. 6:2; Eph. 4:29–32; Col. 3:16; Heb. 10:24–25.

30 2 Peter 3:11–14.

31 Eddie Gibbs, *ChurchNext* (Downers Grove, Ill.: InterVarsity Press, 2000), 220.

32 Eph. 1:18–23.

33 Matt. 6:33.

34 Prov. 4:23.

35 Phil. 4:12–13.

36 Eph. 4:17–24; Rom. 12:1–2.

37 Gal. 6:9–10.

38 Rom. 6:12–13.

Chapter 3: Sources of Popular Culture

1 John Calvin, *Institutes of the Christian Religion,* ed. John T. McNeill, trans. Ford Lewis Battles (Philadelphia: Westminster Press, 1960), 3.14.2.

2 Gen. 1:26–31.

3 Calvin, *Institutes,* 1.15.6.

4 Ibid.

5 Prov. 4:23.

6 Cf. Ps. 104:27–32; Acts 17:25–27.

7 Edmund P. Clowney, *The Church* (Downers Grove, Ill.: InterVarsity Press, 1995), 179.

8 James 1:17; Acts 17:25–27.

9 Ps. 52:1.

10 Matt. 5:45.

11 This idea of living a contented life of gratitude to God is a central theme of Ecclesiastes, as I argue in *Ecclesiastes: Ancient Wisdom When All Else Fails* (Downers Grove, Ill.: InterVarsity Press, 2001).

12 William D. Romanowski, *Eyes Wide Open: Looking for God in Popular Culture* (Grand Rapids: Brazos Press, 2001), 47.

13 Cf. David Remnick, "Birthday Boy," *The New Yorker,* May 14, 2001, 102ff.

14 Kenneth A. Myers, *All God's Children and Blue Suede Shoes* (Wheaton, Ill.: Crossway, 1989), xiii.

15 Cf. Ps. 73:21–22.

16 Gal. 5:16–23.

17 Rom. 7:14–23; 1:18–23.

18 Cf. Agnieszka Tennant, "Possessed or Obsessed?" in *Christianity Today,* September 3, 2001, 66ff.

19 For a full discussion of this passage, see *Findings,* fall 2001.

20 Rom. 1:21–32.

21 Gen. 6:3; Acts 14:17; 17:26–27.

Chapter 4: Judging Popular Culture

1 Frank Burch Brown, *Good Taste, Bad Taste, and Christian Taste* (Oxford: Oxford University Press, 2000), 58.

2 Readers familiar with H. Richard Niebuhr's *Christ and Culture* (New York: Harper and Row, 1951, 1975) will have recognized thus far elements of several of his explanations of how the church approaches culture. One who follows a kingdom approach to popular

culture will insist that Christ must transform culture, but that, in the process, He must stand in and over it.

3 Kenneth A. Myers, *All God's Children and Blue Suede Shoes* (Wheaton, Ill.: Crossway, 1989), 30.

4 Cf. Ps. 82.

5 Matt. 7:1; 1 Cor. 4:5.

6 Eph. 4:14.

7 1 Cor. 3:10–13.

8 Arthur C. Danto, *Art after the End of Art* (Princeton: Princeton University Press, 1997), 12.

9 Prov. 3:5–6; 14:12; Jer. 17:9.

10 1 Chron. 12:32; Acts 17:16–34.

11 1 John 4:1–3.

12 Ps. 11:4–6.

13 Col. 3:17; 1 Cor. 10:31; Acts 5:29.

14 Ps. 19:1–6; 2 Tim. 3:15–17.

15 Cf. Pss. 111:2; 36:9.

16 Ps. 111:2; Col. 3:16.

17 Cf. Dürer's writings on painting and human proportion in *The Writings of Albrecht Dürer,* trans. and ed. William Martin Conway (New York: Philosophical Library, 1958).

18 Ibid., 176.

19 W. H. Gardner, ed., *Gerard Manley Hopkins: Poems and Prose* (London: Penguin Books, 1985), 98.

20 This is why Reformed churches, for example, put so much emphasis on confessions of faith and other kinds of creedal formulas. Without such artifacts of tradition to guide our thinking about the Word of God and the life of faith, we run the risk of being pulled aside from truth into error.

21 No, Thomas Kinkade did not invent the use of brilliant light in painting.

22 Brown, *Good Taste, Bad Taste, and Christian Taste,* xi.

23 Ibid., xiii.

24 Ibid., 23.

Chapter 5: Approaching Popular Culture

1 Douglas John Hall, *The End of Christendom and the Future of Christianity* (Valley Forge, Pa.: Trinity Press International, 1995), 65-66.

2 Eph. 5:15-16.

3 Ps. 14:1.

4 Prov. 3:5-6.

5 Eph. 4:17-24.

6 1 Peter 1:13; 2 Cor. 10:3-5.

7 Phil. 4:6-7.

8 Cf. Ps. 143.

9 Ps. 90:12.

10 Ps. 36:9.

11 James 1:5-8.

12 1 Tim. 2:1-3.

13 Gen. 6:3; Ps. 19:1-6; Rom. 1:18-21.

14 Ps. 52:1-4; Acts 14:17; Acts 17:24-28.

15 Col. 4:2-3; Eph. 1:18.

16 Ps. 83:16.

17 Cf. Harry Blamires, *The Christian Mind* (Ann Arbor: Servant, 1978), and Mark A. Noll, *The Scandal of the Evangelical Mind* (Grand Rapids: Eerdmans, 1994).

18 James Sire, *Habits of the Mind* (Downers Grove, Ill.: InterVarsity Press, 2000).

19 1 Peter 1:13.

20 Sire, *Habits of the Mind,* 65.

21 Jonathan Edwards, "Christian Knowledge," in *The Works of Jonathan Edwards,* ed. Edward Hickman (Edinburgh: Banner of Truth, 1995), 2:157.

22 Ibid., 159.

23 Ibid., 162-63.

24 Cf. Myron Magnet, *The Dream and the Nightmare* (New York: William Morrow and Company, 1993).

25 Psalm 141 is a particularly relevant prayer to use in preparing for such an outing.

26 Acts 17:16–17.

27 Prov. 27:17.

28 Prov. 3:5–6.

29 Matt. 5:43–48; Phil. 2:12–13; 1 Cor. 10:31.

30 1 Cor. 9:19–23.

31 Prov. 11:30.

Chapter 6: Moments of Transcendence

1 Graham Cray, "Through Popular Music: 'Wholly Holy'?" in *Beholding the Glory,* ed. Jeremy Begbie (Grand Rapids: Baker, 2000), 119.

2 Kenneth A. Myers, *All God's Children and Blue Suede Shoes* (Wheaton, Ill.: Crossway, 1989), xiii.

3 Cf. 1 Sam. 23:8–39; 1 Chron. 11:10–47.

4 1 Chron. 12:23–38.

5 William D. Romanowski, *Eyes Wide Open: Looking for God in Popular Culture* (Grand Rapids: Brazos Press, 2001), 16.

6 Phil. 4:8.

7 Cf. Mark 6:34.

8 John 3:16; Phil. 2:5–11.

9 Gal. 3:1.

10 William D. Romanowski, *Pop Culture Wars* (Downers Grove, Ill.: InterVarsity Press, 1996), 306.

11 Eph. 4:14.

12 Eph. 4:17–24; Rom. 12:1–2.

13 1 Cor. 3:21–23.

14 Romanowski, *Eyes Wide Open,* 71.

15 For information about how you or your church can become involved in a sports ministry, call Butch Garman at Cedar Springs Church, 865-693-9331.

16 Mark 6:31.

17 1 Tim. 4:8.

18 Jonathan Edwards, "The Christian Pilgrim," in *The Works of Jonathan Edwards*, ed. Edward Hickman (Edinburgh: Banner of Truth, 1995), 2:244.

19 Robert K. Johnston, *Reel Spirituality* (Grand Rapids: Baker, 2000), 69.

20 Ps. 105:4.

21 Ps. 37:4-6.

22 Cf. Pss. 59, 69, etc.

23 1 Thess. 5:18; Ps. 4:6-7.

24 Acts 1:7.

25 Romanowski, *Eyes Wide Open*, 71, 81.

26 Cf. Ps. 81:13-15.

261
M8245R
LINCOLN CHRISTIAN COLLEGE AND SEMINARY
118638

T. M. Moore is pastor of teaching ministries at Cedar Springs Church in Knoxville, Tennessee. He is a graduate of the University of Missouri (B.A.) and Reformed Theological Seminary (M.Div., M.C.E.), and has pursued additional studies at the University of Pretoria, the University of Miami, and the University of Wales.

He is a fellow of the Wilberforce Forum and editor of their online journal, *Findings*. His column, Ars Musica et Poetica, appears on the *BreakPoint* Webpage, along with his daily devotionals. He is North American editor for Scripture Union Publications, a ministry associate with Reformation and Revival Ministries and the Jonathan Edwards Institute, and associate editor of *Reformation and Revival Journal*.

Moore is also the author of several books, including *I Will Be Your God: How God's Covenant Enriches Our Lives* (P&R). His book *Ecclesiastes* (IVP) received a 2002 Award of Merit from *Christianity Today*. His essays, reviews, articles, and poetry have appeared in numerous journals and periodicals. He is a frequent speaker in churches, conferences, and seminars.

He and his wife, Susie, have four children and ten grandchildren, and make their home in Concord, Tennessee. When he is not working, T. M. wiles away the time listening to Celtic music, reading poetry, playing the mountain dulcimer, and enjoying the glory of God in creation.

$11.99
3 4711 00181 4898